FINDING GOD IN A BROKEN WORLD

JOHN R. CLARKE

authorHOUSE®

AuthorHouse™
1663 Liberty Drive
Bloomington, IN 47403
www.authorhouse.com
Phone: 1 (800) 839-8640

Published by AuthorHouse 12/10/2015

ISBN: 978-1-5049-2124-4 (sc)
ISBN: 978-1-5049-2125-1 (e)

Print information available on the last page.

TABLE OF CONTENTS

DEDICATION

This book is dedicated to our Heavenly Father the Almighty and everlasting God, to our Lord and Saviour Jesus Christ and to the blessed anointing of the Holy Spirit who is our comforter and teacher. May you the reader, receive grace and peace and find many blessings among the pages of this book.

I also dedicate this book to my wonderful wife Kalpna and our son Sam, both of whom are a great gift and blessing from God.

Preface

There is no doubt that we are entering the final stages of the history of this world. Lawlessness abounds, terrorism is on the increase, wars and rumors of wars, volcanic eruptions, cyclones, floods and tornados are also becoming more common as the earth struggles under the burden of mankind's rebellion. So what does the future hold for the beloved of Christ? *Finding God in a broken world* provides insight into the steps to remaining free in Christ, during the turbulent days ahead, in a world that is in rebellion and hostile to everything that is central to the Christian life.

The book is aimed at Christians at all stages of their relationship with Christ and should also be of interest for those who are seeking to understand the basis of victorious Christian living.

The book explores seven key areas to the victorious Christian life and remaining free in Christ regardless of the circumstances we find ourselves facing in the coming days. As Christians, we are either afraid of or want to skip over quickly the challenging teachings in the word of

God, such as the struggles with and consequences of sin, and the coming wrath of God, in order to reach the more positive teachings on salvation and eternal life for all who believe in Jesus as Lord and Saviour. However, we shouldn't be afraid to confront the thought provoking teachings, as these brings God's purpose of salvation and plans for eternity into perspective. In this book I have tried to provide this viewpoint in order to show the exciting assurances of God's plan for each one of His children as we move toward the end of time.

Therefore, this book contain some thoughts about the consequences of sin and the hurts and pain that they may cause in our lives, and how our past experiences may hinder God's purpose for our lives and prevent us from being the people God created us to be. The early part of the book also focuses on the undeniable love of God for mankind and for His children. In the second part of the book I have concentrated on the very positive and exciting consequences of living life to His fullness, in overcoming the world to reach His purposes for our lives and in moving forward in victorious living before the Lord in these end times. It is my hope and prayer that you will be inspired, comforted and blessed by the reading of this book.

John R Clarke

1

EMBRACING THE LOVE OF GOD

Love is central to human existence, we all desire and crave love and affection. We all love to read or to watch on television a really good love story with a happy ending. When people fall in love and get married, everyone wishes to see the bride and groom live happy ever after. Humans are capable of giving a great deal of love and affection and long to be loved in return. There are endless stories of people sacrificing a great deal for a loved one, whether it is a parent giving up an organ or some other great sacrifice for their child, or even the ultimate sacrifice of giving up their lives to save a loved one from death.

Many struggle or in some cases cannot live without love. Indeed, it appears that love is required in increasing abundance nowadays to enable people to cope with the demands of this 21st century world we live in.

However, is modern love failing? In the Western World statistics tell us that there is a growing divorce rate, breakdown of relationships are higher than ever and more people than ever before are turning to alternatives to meet their basic human needs, such as anti-depressants, alcohol or drugs, as a form of escapism in a world they struggle to cope with. There were 851,000 divorces and annulments of marriages in the US in 2012.[1] The use of antidepressants in the United Kingdom has soared by 500% in the last 20 years, and over the same time period, the use of anti-depressants has increased by 20% each year across Europe.[2] If love is all the world needs and wants, then it is clearly not working. Or is it? Maybe we need to revisit what love is and get a clearer definition of what we mean when we talk about love.

What is love?

How do we define love? What do we mean when we tell someone we love them? Scientists tell us that love results from a combination of chemical reactions. Love begins in the brain when we think about someone or something we are attracted to or love and, chemicals called neurotransmitters (the scientific terms are adrenaline, dopamine and serotonin) are all released, and these cause other hormones called vasopressin and oxytocin to be released also. These chemicals basically make us feel good.[3] But is that really all love is? A bunch of chemicals floating around and making us feel good? What does it mean that God loved the world?[4] Is love more than just a chemical reaction? Interestingly, the same cluster of chemicals can be released when people love other things, for example, cats dogs, or even cars, and if people feel the same way about their animals and cars as people do when they love a partner, then in some instances they experience the same chemical reaction that make people in love feel so good.

There is the infatuation we sometimes see when two people connect with one another and fall in love, they want to be with each other all the time, when they are apart they are thinking of each other, and they count the hours to when they will be together again. They can't help talking to their friends about the love of their life. They just enjoy being together more than anything else in the world. They do nice things for each other, they go out for a romantic candle lit dinner, or stroll in the park. They become best friends, and share all kinds of secrets, and get to know each other really well. Does this type of love endure, and is it a lasting love? Yes it can be because some people remain in love for the rest of their lives. Some talk about finding their soul mate, or their other half, or the love of their life, and love can be enduring.

So what is love and what does it mean to want to be loved? We want someone who accepts us, who wants to be with us, who respects us even when they have seen the worst side of us. We look for a soul mate, someone who shares the same interests, goals and desires we have for life. Somebody to spend time with and someone we can grow old with. Does love end here or is there more?

What happens when the relationship doesn't work out, and there is the pain of breaking up, or causing the home to fall apart.

The problem of worldly love

As we have already discussed, love is central to the deepest need of man. From the moment we are born to the moment we die, and everything in between, we long for a deep and satisfying love. Men and women throughout the world are infatuated with love, just think of all the popular songs that are written about love, and all the romantic movies that can be found on our televisions and at the movies. We long to be loved and accepted and we fear rejection above everything else.

However, many of us have suffered rejection at some time in our lives by someone who we dearly wanted to love us. Perhaps the most painful rejection is when our parents or a partner reject us. This can lead to us developing a poor image about love and unfortunately ourselves. This can affect our ability to achieve the most basic of needs, the need for love and acceptance. Our ability to accept love and to feel that we are worthy of being loved can be especially difficult if the rejection comes from our earthly father. Even worse is having suffered at the hands of an abusive earthly father or family member. The sense of loss and guilt that can be experienced through an absent father, due to any circumstance, can deeply affect our ability to accept love from others, though the deep need for love remains. Such experiences can leave the victim confused and they may find it difficult to believe that they are entitled to receive a deep, loving and meaningful relationship in its deepest form. Even for those who have not experienced such trauma, profound questions remain with so many divorces occurring in Christian and secular marriages alike. Can our intense need for love be met in this fallen world we live in? Yet there is something that drives us ever forward to try and find love and meaning in the world we live in.

God's love for the world

When God talks about loving the world, does He just want to spend time with it? No of course not, it is much deeper and heartfelt than just hanging out. Probably, the most quoted verse in the entire Bible has to do with the love of God and the sacrifice that God made for His beloved world.[4] The truth is that we can find the love and acceptance we long for by looking for love in the right place and that place is God. The truth is that God looks for us and longs to provide for our every need. He wants us to receive His unconditional love and He also wants to receive love from us. God loved the world so much, and that is the key: His love for the world is immeasurable. We cannot imagine just how much God loves each and every one of us. He loved us so much that He was prepared to make the ultimate sacrifice on our behalf by substituting His only Son to take our place for everything we have done wrong and for everything we deserve punishment for.

Through God's love for us we can have a new beginning, we can start all over again. When we accept God's love by accepting Jesus into our lives, we move from being an enemy of God, and from being separated from a heavenly Father's love and acceptance, into a place where we have forgiveness, acceptance and a place in God's own family. No matter what our experiences are, what rejections and abuse we may have received during our childhood and as adults, God loves us and wants to be a part of our lives. God wants to exchange our broken experiences for His perfect love.

> *God loves us as we are and He wants us to love Him in return. God does not reject us but longs to put His arms around us and fill us with His love.*

A loving God in a broken world

Our experiences of life have shaped who we are and can leave us with many questions, perhaps the biggest question of all is, why God? Why has a loving God allowed this to happen to me? Why didn't God intervene? Why didn't God stop this from happening? Why did God allow millions of people to be massacred in wars or genocide attacks, why did God not answer prayers and allow a baby to die or a loving parent to die young? Why does a loving God allow murder to continue every day? The questions can be endless and the answers difficult to find. In fact over the centuries such observations have no doubt turned many away from God. Sometimes people turn away from God in bitterness or even hatred, because they hold God responsible for their loss, or for not answering their prayers in the way they wanted or hoped for, or they simply cannot accept that a loving God would not intervene to stop the wickedness and evil that is evident in the world. They are not alone. The prophet Habakkuk wrote about the very same issues that face us today.[5] How long shall we cry out for justice when there appears to be none? How long do we cry out against the violence and destruction we see every day?

Indeed, many people have rejected the thought that there can be a fair and loving God based on the violence they have seen and experienced in the world, thinking that God has somehow failed. However, God answered Habakkuk's cry for justice to come upon the wicked and ultimately God will answer the cries for justice around the world. He will administer His perfect justice to all people who have carried out evil acts. The Saints in heaven ask how much longer O Lord before you avenge the bloodshed that they have suffered because they believed in the Lord Jesus Christ?[6] The answer to the cries for justice is just a little while longer before the wrath of God is poured out on all men and women for their violence and iniquities.

Where was God when I needed him the most? The answer is He was in exactly the same place as He was when His beloved Son died on the cross. He was in heaven on His throne aware of everything that was happening. God grieved when we grieved, God hurt when we hurt.

The answer to the question why doesn't God put an end all the suffering in the world lies at the beginning of the story of mankind in the Garden of Eden. Adam and Eve disobeyed God and the consequences for mankind were enormous. Firstly death entered the world, then separation from God, expulsion from paradise, and mankind acquired knowledge that we were never meant to have because we weren't equipped to handle it. The innocence of mankind disappeared and it wasn't very long before murder entered the world.

Adam and Eve had a choice to either obey or disobey God The choice for every man and woman today remains the same, do we believe God or don't we? Why did God put the tree of knowledge of good and evil in the centre of the Garden of Eden in the first place? Because God wanted His children and mankind to have a free choice to obey Him. The presence of the tree showed us one very important spiritual principal, we are free to make choices and the choices we make have consequences. We are free to decide if we will obey God which is right or to disobey God which is wrong. Both actions have consequences and those consequences affect not only our own lives but the lives of others. It has resulted in a people who are hurt, angry, often struggling to cope with what life throws at them, and most of all a people who are separated from God.

The account of what happened in the Garden of Eden at the beginning of time teaches us several things about our relationship with God. Firstly, God trusted us and gave us a free will to choose between life and death. We were in control of our lives from the outset and we were free to choose as we are today whether to believe what God tells us or to reject it and go our own way. Secondly, the presence of the tree of knowledge of good and evil showed us that temptation was present for mankind from the very beginning. This means that we are faced with a choice of doing the right or wrong thing on a day-to-day basis, and the choices we make in life may result from time-to-time in being wrong. The third thing that it teaches us, is that temptation and evil starts in the mind. When Eve considered the fruit, although she knew it was forbidden by God, she saw how attractive the fruit was and how desirable it was for gaining wisdom so she ate it and also gave it to her husband. Why didn't Adam intervene on behalf of Eve? Probably, because he also saw how attractive the fruit was and knew he wanted wisdom. Why did they eat the fruit? Possibly because they wanted to be like God. We want to be gods in our own right. A lot of the opposition to God in the world derives from mankind wanting to be free to do whatever they want to and not be accountable for their actions.

The fourth thing that this account teaches us, is that to disobey God has dire consequences for us as individuals and collectively as the human race. However, unpopular it is with modern thought the truth is that God's nature demands that He punishes sin. Fifthly and most importantly despite mankind's' rebellion in the Garden of Eden, God still loved us and provided a way that we could be reconciled with Him. God's love for mankind is greater than His revulsion at our sin and drove Him to make provision for us by substituting His only Son and placing Him on the cross in our place. God has provided a way back for us out of His love. The question remains will we accept what He has provided for us, the choice is ours.

God's new plan for the world

God has a tremendous almost unbelievable love and He had a plan B that would enable mankind to return to Him and be accepted as one of His children. God is so rich in mercy and He loves us so much that even though we were spiritually dead and doomed to death through our sinful actions, He gave us our lives back again. The truth is that God loves us more than we can hope and imagine and He wants us to love Him back. God sent Jesus because He wants us to be a part of His family and He wants to call us His sons and daughters.

> **God loves us so much that He made a
> way for us to be right with Him through
> accepting Jesus as our Lord and Saviour.**

So we come back to the question, why does a good God allow evil things to happen to good people? When God created the world, He looked and saw that it was good and he was pleased with what He had created. Then evil entered the world in the shape of a serpent and led mankind into sin and rebellion against God and that led to the death of mankind both in a spiritual and physical sense. However, the death of mankind was never in God's original plan but as a consequence of sin, mankind was barred from paradise. God had a choice to make, to destroy mankind and that would mean all mankind through all the generations and start all over again or to allow sin to continue until it finally ran its course and came to maturity. God chose the latter and the clues to why He did that are scattered throughout the Bible.

One of the clearest examples of God's plan is found in the parable of the wheat and the tares.[7] The evil tares and the good wheat grow up side by side. We all know that the field is the world, the good seed are Christians, the enemy who sowed tares is the devil, the harvest is the end of the age and the reapers are the angels.

The point being is that once God decided to continue with mankind after our rebellion, He had to allow mankind to run his course. That meant allowing those who are evil to continue alongside those who are good. As the wheat grew with the tares it is sometimes impossible to tell the difference between the two until they are fully grown. Also those who may appear to be tares in their youth may turn out to be wheat. If the Lord had of come 10, 20, 30, 40 or even 50 or more years ago would we have been saved? God has given us free choice and He must allow the free choice of mankind to continue its path until the end of this age. That means that both evil and good men will stand side by side in this world. God is patient and He is waiting to enable everyone to have a chance of repentance and to come into His Kingdom and be saved. That is why evil still exists in the world and is not simply blotted out of existence by God, because while there is the remotest chance of people repenting and being saved, God will wait. An important point often missed in this parable is that good and evil are not just existing side by side but are growing and maturing. So the atrocities and the evil will worsen but men of God will also grow in character and power as we move toward the end of this world

God doesn't rush things He waits until the time is right. God is patient and it's not His desire to see anyone perish and He hopes that all men will come to repentance and be saved.[8] God is perfect in His timing but allows evil to continue for the time being. God won't wait forever and there will be a time when God will say;-it's time for my wrath and anger to be poured out on the world.

> **God never rushes things His timing
> is always the right time.**

We are shocked at what we see on our television screens, the genocide, the blatant murder and the justification of murder, the hideous crimes that men and women do every day, all of which can be traced back to the fall of mankind. Yes they are becoming more violent and unbelievably evil and the days of lawlessness will continue until Christ comes again. Once evil has run its course, there is no more time for men and women to repent. Time is up.

So after mankind's' rebellion in the Garden of Eden, why didn't God just start over from the beginning? I believe the reason rests in the Ephesians chapter 1 verse 4 which tells us that God chose us before He created the world and He created us to be Holy and blameless before Him. If God had already created us before the foundation of the world and if He destroyed Adam and Eve after eating the forbidden fruit, then He would have had to destroy the whole of mankind which would have included all of those of us who hadn't yet been born. However, God's love shone through and He so loved His world and the people in it past, present and future that He persevered and found a solution to the problem of mankind. That solution was to send His only Son Jesus into the world to die in our place, that whoever believed in Him would not perish, as our sins deserve but have everlasting life.

God's provision

God loves us and has made provision for us through His son Jesus Christ. This was so that we would be able to see just how vast God's love for us is and when we grasp the extent of this reality then we begin to understand and allow God to completely fill us with His love.[9] The truth is that God's love for us surpasses our understanding and expectations and is beyond our wildest dreams or hopes.[9] We are very important to God, no matter what we have experienced, no matter what disappointments we have encountered or what we have suffered, we are loved by God and that love is able to bring healing into every situation. If we allow God access to our lives and especially to the places in our hearts that hurt the most, God's love will penetrate and bring healing. God loves us with a perfect love that does not demand anything in return, other than we accept His Son into our lives as our Lord and Saviour. God wants to bless us, restore us and to make His face shine upon us.[10]

However desperate our situation is today and regardless of the deep hurts of our past, God offers His unconditional love to us today and forever more. He can meet our deepest needs right now and bring inner healing where we need it the most. Will we give God access to our vulnerable places and let Him bring healing? Will we truly open our hearts to Him today and allow Him in?

> **Nothing can separate us from the love of God. If God is for us, nothing that is against us can prevail.[11]**

So great is God's love for us, that nothing can separate us from it. Indeed, death, life, angels, principalities, powers, Governments, nothing in this present life, nor anything in the future, no problem or obstacle however vast, nothing in the whole of creation can separate us from the love of God which can be found through our Lord Jesus Christ.[11]

God has a deep, deep love for us that nothing can separate us from. Why has God allowed bad things to happen to us? Because He wants us to use those hurtful experiences to help others who have suffered similar trials. God has given mankind the gift of free will and that means we can use that free will to do good, or to do evil. It is God's hope that we will allow Him to shape our suffering into something that will bring glory to His name and to help others that do not yet know Him

It is not our fault that adverse things have happened to us, rather these things have happened so that God can be glorified. We are special to God and all the experiences we encounter are important to God, nothing goes unnoticed. God cares deeply about us and He desires to heal our wounds and set us free to be the people He created us to be. Nothing is too difficult for Him nor is any circumstance beyond His reach. God is love and He desires to bring that love into our lives. Will we allow him to do that? He desires that we are made whole. Will we give Him access to those areas of our life that need healing? Will we allow Him access to the memories that have caused us so much pain and allow Him to set us free?

What is God's purpose for our lives? It is to be transformed into His likeness. We are called to be changed into God's likeness through the renewal of our minds so that our minds are fixed on God and receiving His thoughts as much as human minds can grasp the great thoughts of God.[12] Once are minds are transformed and focused on God then we begin to see what God's perfect will and plan is for our lives. We can begin to be excited by what God wants to do for us and through us.[12]

Changing our thinking

When we begin to share some of God's thoughts a whole new Spiritual world opens up to us and there are endless possibilities as we begin to partake in God's plan for our lives, for our families lives, for our churches, for our Governments. God's aim for each and every one of His family is that they are transformed into the likeness of His Son. To allow God to change our minds is the highest form of worship because it affects our inner most being. So often we are what we think. If we think negatively then we open ourselves up to a life full of negatives. God loves us so much that He wants to change us, which is why He gave us His word, so that by prayerfully reading the Bible and allowing its teaching to penetrate into the areas of our lives that need changing, we can be transformed. How we think about things and respond to our innermost thoughts are largely responsible for where we are in our lives. For example, if people who are diagnosed with a serious illness are told there is no hope and they have a limited time to live they will often succumb and die within that time period. Our thought life is a battleground and being in control of the battleground is vital for Christian living.

Let this thought change our hearts, God loves us but He loves us too much to allow us to remain as we are. God is both patient and gentle in the way He changes us. We may not believe that God has changed us much but He has been working and He hasn't given up on us, each one of us are His work in progress. Surrender the things that trouble us to Him and He will heal those memories, disappointments and betrayals. Then we can begin to receive the love of God that passes all understanding into our hearts. We may not have received all that God has for us yet but we can begin to press on toward the goal for which God has called us. With God beside us helping us, there is always an opportunity to leave the past behind and move forward to a new and exciting life.

Why does God love us so much?

As with human love God wants a relationship with us, He wants to be our God and He wants us for His people.[13] He wants to share His thoughts with us and He wants us to share our excitement, our frustrations, our disappointments, our worries and our pain with Him. Sometimes it is enough to just come into His presence and escape from the world for a while, to be quiet and still and receive His love and His healing for our damaged minds and souls. To get away to a special place and to receive His love and to give what little love we have to offer. God longs for us to get to know Him and to share in the things that He has planned for us. There is a big part of us that needs the love of God, and He has promised to fill that longing in us when we accept Him and enter into a relationship with His Son Jesus. Yet, for those who already have that relationship we need to continue to make time to be in love and to receive love from the living God. Life can be very busy and there are a number of demands on our time which may mean there simply not enough hours in the day. However, we should always make time for God.

What is love? Love is patient, kind, is not envious, it doesn't promote selfishness but has the other person's best interests at heart, it doesn't keep a record of all the wrongs and bad things that have happened, love is truthful, love doesn't delight in getting its own back or hitting out for revenge, love isn't rude, love is protective, has great hope, and never gives up no matter what has happened.[14] God is love.[15]

A short prayer.

Dear loving heavenly Father thank you that you love us and allow us to be who we are. Thank you that there are no limits to your love for us and that no matter what our experiences have been up until now, you have a purpose for our lives. You have never let go of us and nothing can separate us from your love. May we surrender the areas of our lives that need your special touch and allow you to heal our memories and our emotions. May you graciously make us whole and be the people you created us to be. In Jesus name we ask, Amen

2

FINDING GOD'S PURPOSE FOR OUR LIVES

Planning for the future

We all have plans and dreams, for example, to plan for a vacation, maybe to a place we have never been before. We may have seen the photos of our holiday destination, or even seen a television programme, or a video of the destination, or maybe we have been online to find out about the destination. Once we have made plans and booked the vacation we can get quite excited, we start counting the days until we go, and it is certainly something to look forward too. Alternatively, we might be planning a career move, or looking forward to a possible promotion within the organization we work for. We start to think about what it would be like to be the boss or we think about what is needed to fulfil our ambition and our goals for life. Some might be planning to move home, get a larger house, to move to a better neighbourhood, or to move closer to family or friends. We starting looking at the neighbourhood we want to move too, check house prices in the area to work out if we can afford to move. We go to the real estate agents to see what is available, take a drive around the area, go view the house or apartment, even put in an offer on a property. Some might be planning to start a family, or an addition to the existing family, this can lead to excitement, and maybe a few concerns about whether it will all go well and how they might cope once the new addition arrives.

We may be planning to simply escape our current situation or circumstances, to get out to something better, to move on, or simply run away. Some may simply wish that the world would stop for a while to give them time to recuperate, recharge their batteries and get going again. Some may be planning to stop an addiction or to lose a few pounds. Whatever we are planning or dreaming about it is invariably for something better and we all have hopes and dreams that things will change for the better and be an improvement on our current situation. Even if the change is only temporary, as is the case with a vacation. For some our plans may not be for us but for our children or our partners. May be our partner will get a better job or our children will pass an examination or get better grades or even get into the College of their choice. Whatever we plan for we should always include God and through prayer share our plans with Him and seek His guidance.[1]

Sometimes things don't go to plan, there are setbacks, and we end up discouraged or disillusioned. We may question the wisdom of the plan or be angry at the outcome. We may feel helpless that our life is no longer under our control. How we react in these circumstances will either enable us to succeed or fail. Our reactions and how we deal with setbacks is very important to shaping our future and ultimately in defining the people we will become. Sometimes God in His wisdom will bring us back to the same point as He gently removes the flaw or obstacle in our character that is preventing us from maturing and becoming the people we were created to be. God persists in bringing us back to the same place, because He wants to see us made whole, without flaws, and He wants to complete His work in us. During these testing times it is vital that we never give up no matter what setbacks have occurred, try again, and start all over may be with a modified plan or with a whole new plan. There is always hope for the future and room for optimism.

Trust the Lord that He is in control, and that His timing is perfect. No matter what we face, we will come out stronger, more blessed and wiser from the experience,

God has plans for us

God has plans for our lives too and the plans may not always be plain sailing even with God at the helm of our lives.[2] It may seem at times that God's plan isn't all that good or even working the way we would like it to or hope it would. It may even seem that God is very slow in carrying out His plan. Sometimes we can't see what God is doing, nothing seems to be happening when we desperately want things to move. Stop, wait and allow God to move on our behalf, for if we rush hastily into something then invariably we will mess things up. However, even if this occurs, God has a way of bringing us back to where He wants us to be. He has promised that we have a hope and a future and God keeps His promises.[2]

What are God's purposes for His people?

God's purpose for mankind is that He wants a people who are set aside and dedicated to Him.[3] God wants to be our God and He wants us to be His people, this is the theme that runs right through the Bible, and is central to our understanding of who we are and where we are going in our journey through life. Once we have given our lives to Christ, and have called upon Him as our Lord and Saviour, then we enter into God's family and that is when the excitement really starts. God created man in order to have a relationship with him. From the very beginnings God came down from heaven into the Garden of Eden to walk with Adam in the coolness of the evening.[4] God set aside time to walk with Adam, to have a friendship and a relationship with mankind, among the creation that He had made and that He thought was good. The

Lord still wants that relationship with us today, nothing has changed in that respect.

God has plans for each one of us and God's plan for us is good and full of hope.[2] Sometimes it is difficult for us to see His plan when we consider the challenges we find ourselves facing on a day-to-day basis. Life can seem a struggle at times and at other times it seems that we are on a high. Regardless of whether we are on a high or a low ebb in our life, God is always there and He is the one person we can turn too and rely upon no matter what we are experiencing. God provides us with the stability we require. Part of living is that God tests us to see what is in our heart[5] and to move us forward in Him, and while at times it is difficult to see what God is doing, He knows what is best for us and has our very best interests at heart. Even when we stray far from the path that God would have us tread, He has a way of bringing us back to where He wants us to be.

The Bible tells us that Jesus is the same yesterday, today and forever[6] therefore He knows where we are and where we are going. The Lord can see into the future and He isn't surprised by what lies ahead for us whether that be plain sailing and calm seas or a storm and turbulent seas. It is reassuring to know that the Lord is always there for us. Even when we fall away and are tempted by the world, and by all our ambitions, the Lord gently bring us back on to His path. The wonderful part of bringing us back to where we should be is that we are restored to being at the centre of His will for our lives again. No matter how badly we mess up, the Lord waits patiently for us to return to Him, and He runs to meet us on that road.[7]

God is in control and we can trust Him and depend upon Him.

At times we can be a long way of the track and way out of the will of God. We sometimes ignore the warning signs and even try to justify why we are heading in the direction we are going. At times the Lord lets us go the wrong way just to strengthen our relationship with Him. He can appear distant and withdrawn from us and we can feel lost and alone. There is nothing new about those feelings of loneliness because the disciples and no doubt endless generations since have often had struggles even when they were clearly following the Lord's instructions.[8]

Walking in the Lord's way

Even when we are following the Lord's direction storms and opposition can come.[8] These storms may lead us to question whether we have heard correctly. However, it is important to see them for what they are, storms, which will pass eventually and the sun will return to our lives.

However, before embarking on an important project or at the beginning of very new day, we should always ask for a word from the Lord a Bible verse or passage just for reassurance that we are at the centre of His will. The importance of the word from the Lord is that it enables us to stand in the dark hours before the dawn and the breakthrough that comes with the morning light. The Bible verse, whatever it may be for our situation or particular circumstance provides confidence that we have heard Him correctly, and then we can continue moving forward despite the tempest or discouragements.

I believe that part of building on rock rather than sand[9] is to be armed with the word of God, and to have a word from the Lord enables us to withstand the onslaught, and get through to the other side however intense and thunderous the weather. Indeed, the Bible verse that the Lord gives at the beginning of a new adventure may be the difference between success and failure, in arriving at the other side of the lake, or merely being blown backwards and ending up back where we started.[8]

Hindrances to God's plan

There are two things that are central in God's will for our lives. Firstly, that we have free will[10] and therefore we are free to decide either to do what is right or what is wrong, the choice is ours. The problem with choices is that which is the correct choice is not always clear and sometimes we can embark on the wrong path. In my experience sometimes we can truly believe what we are doing is correct, and we have peace that we are following God's ways. However, in the cold light of day we find out to our cost that we have not taken the right path. At other times we know what we are about to do is clearly wrong and we deliberately out of disobedience continue anyway. God has to deal with the sin in us, whether that sin is deliberate disobedience, or whether it is not doing what we should through ignorance. God has a way of drawing us back into His will whether it is in a spectacular way, such as the way God dealt with Jonah[11], or by a more subtle approach by gently drawing us to where He wants us to be.

Sometimes we lose our way and feel that God is far from us and even fret that he has left us. May be we do something that we consider so awful that we struggle to forgive ourselves and are unable to receive God's forgiveness.

Secondly the Bible tells us how God has responded to our sin and rebellion.[12] Even though our sins are like scarlet, God can make us become white as snow.[12] The condition for God's favour is that we willingly accept Jesus as our Lord and Saviour, and once we have done that we are called to willingly follow His ways. We are called to be obedient and be a part of His family[13]

> **The Lord has provided a way for us to return to Him when we have strayed or miss the mark. Even though our sins are like crimson in His sight, He wants to cleanse us and make us Holy as He is Holy.**[12]

There is something very secure about being part of God's family. We have an identity, a place to belong and a place where we are accepted and loved and cherished.

God has brought us into His family and all believers in Christ are your brothers and sisters which is good news indeed. However, for those who reject Christ as the Son of the Living God there lays another path.[14]

Which path do we follow?

There are two types of people on the earth, those that love Jesus, and those that despise Jesus. For those that love the Lord their destiny is to spend eternity in heaven with God.[15] The day that we accept Jesus as our Lord and Saviour, and believe that He has taken our place on the cross for our sins, that is the day that we start our journey towards heaven. For those who reject God's Son there is a different path and that path ends up in hell.[13] The whole concept of hell and eternal damnation is not popular with 21st century theologians but the Bible teaches it and I believe it.

Perhaps one of the most disappointing aspects of the Western World during the current climate of recession is that men and women prefer to stay in their evil ways rather than returning to God. In the United Kingdom at this time, families are struggling to make ends meet, many have become unemployed with no prospect of a job on the horizon, and many of our young people have no prospect of ever getting a meaningful job. Despite the hardships there is no evidence that individuals are returning to God. Church attendance is low and there is a growing belief that there is no place for God in modern life, in other words God is outdated and no longer relevant. The interesting fact is that many people who have turned away from God as being irrelevant to 21st century mankind used to go to church and Sunday school when they were younger.

Governments do not know how to solve the current crises and are hoping that somehow the problems of the Western World will rectify themselves. However, I firmly believe the problem lies in mankind's' rebellion against God. Governments have no answers to mankind's' sin, and indeed the Bible tells us that when the time comes for God to deliver His wrath and anger on mankind, the heart breaking fact is that the kings of the earth, the rich, and the poor, the slaves, and the men and women will hide in caves and call on the mountains to fall on them to protect them from the wrath and anger of God.[16] I'm sure that if these people, even at the very end of time, call upon the name of the Lord they could be saved, but mankind preferred darkness to light.[16]

For all who believe in Jesus are brought into God's family and are called His children.[17]

Will everybody be saved?

In the early part of the 21st century there are many views on what happens at the end of the earth and one of the many things that theologians appear divided on is the interpretation of 2 Peter 3:9 which states God is not willing that anyone should perish, but that all should come to repentance and be saved.[18] Some have interpreted this to mean that all mankind regardless of their beliefs and how they have lived on the earth will be in heaven.[19] However, we have to dismiss large parts of the Bible and it's teaching on God's wrath in order to reach that conclusion. The more logical interpretation is that God is waiting for as long as He can before pouring His wrath out upon the earth in the hope that as many men and women that can be saved will be saved. There will become a time when God's judgment will come as surely as the seasons change.[20] There will be a point in history when God will say now is the time, enough is enough. The clock is ticking relentlessly towards that day when we can say come 'Lord Jesus come'.

True believers in Christ

The Bible teaches that there will be a multitude of believers in heaven and there will be so many that it is impossible to count the number.[21] All those who call upon the name of the Lord will be saved,[22] is the good news of the gospel. John in his first letter reassures us that our sins are forgiven for Christ's name sake.[23] We can claim that reassurance and God gives us further assurance of our position as Christians and part of His family by sealing us with the Holy Spirit who is our promise of eternal life.[24] The Holy Spirit is the guarantee that God has not abandoned us or left us as orphans but is here to guide us into the truth of the gospel,[25] as well as our comforter in life.

> *The Holy Spirit is the Lord's guarantee that we are not abandoned and that He is with us until the end of the age.*

God has made plans for us, and assures us that we have a hope and a future with Him.[2] Central to God's plan for our lives is that we fulfil our purpose on the earth and be witnesses to the world of the existence of God and the truth that is the gospel message, that through Jesus, all who believe can have eternal life.[26] Notice the emphasis on all who believe, so that suggests that not everyone is destined for eternal life. The fact that God has plans for us and that we have become part of His family should not be twisted. There is a popular teaching movement among Christians that focuses on God wanting to bless us and make us rich. This is often coupled with giving, sometimes large sums of money, to a named ministry with the promise that God will bless us in return. What is more worrying is they often claim to have a special revelation from God that has to be purchased through an expensive contribution to their ministry. The truth is that if God wants to share something that important He would tell us directly and He doesn't charge for the privilege of knowing something vitally important to all our futures. The claim of special revelation from God, known only to a few privileged individuals, is nothing new as similar claims occurred in the early church.

We should point out that God does bless financially, but our main purpose here on earth is to be witnesses for Him in whatever circumstances He places us in. Those who are obedient to Jesus' teaching are doing the will of God.[27] That is why it is so important to study the Bible and know what it teaches. Remember that Jesus expects us to follow His example.[28] Jesus has also warned us about the world we live in and that we will face the same problems with the world that He did.[29] Therefore, we can expect opposition from the world, and this may mean that we may not be accepted in some circles because of our faith. This can be difficult especially if we are the only Christian in our place of work or in our social circle. It is never easy to be rejected. Take heart, God has placed us where we are for a purpose and nobody else will be able to achieve what we can achieve. Each of us is unique!

True disciples of the Lord Jesus will find that they are in a battle with the forces of darkness.[30] God expects us to stand against the schemes of Satan and has promised to deliver us from the trials we face, not to prevent the trials themselves, but to ensure we can come out the other side as stronger and more functional people than before we started the trial.[31] We are more than conquerors.[32] However, the battles that we face against the enemy are testing grounds for our faith. We need at these times to learn be strong, and to stand against the attack of the enemy, and to persevere in the fight until we can come out victorious. This we do through and with God.

Our purpose for being on the earth is to bring glory to God. It is vitally important that we understand this because if we don't, we are likely to build our lives on sand rather than the rock which is the word of God.

As we have already stated God does want to bless us but that is not His primary purpose for our being here. Our primary purpose is to be God's representatives on the earth and to bring glory to God. To be witnesses for whom God is and what God's kingdom stands for. My concern for Western Christianity is that so often we are too earthly minded to be any heavenly good.

However, the most important part of our lives should centre on our relationship with God. It is important that we develop our relationship with God for we are destined to spend eternity with Him. There is an important passage in Matthew 7:21-23 where people come to the Lord on judgment day, and tell Him that they have done wonderful great things for Him, but the Lord doesn't know who they are. It is our relationship with the Lord that matters not necessarily what we do. We may never be great preachers or great evangelists or even carry out great miracles in the name of Jesus, but we can be a witness for the Lord in the community we live in. We can help our neighbours, we can offer a listening ear to the lonely or the distressed. We can be a witness by our attitude in the workplace, or to our children, our parents or spouses and partners. There is a lot we can do every day by just asking the Lord to lead us to the needy. The Lord is sometimes in the very small things of life and what we do and how we do these things can make a huge difference in the world we live in.

However, our faith does need to be accompanied by good deeds which should be our motivation in serving the Lord. It goes without saying that developing a relationship with the Lord by spending time regularly in prayer and in studying His word is more important to God than performing great miracles in front of men. The Lord wants to be an important part of our lives, He wants to be a part of the decisions we make. The Lord wants to be invited into our lives and be a part of our victories, our joys and our failures. The Lord wants to help, yet in this busy world which demands so much of our time we often forget the most important person in our life and that is our Lord and Saviour Jesus Christ.

As we develop our friendship and relationship with Him our love will grow and we will be able to put into perspective our daily experiences of life whether they be good or bad. A relationship with the Lord Jesus brings with it many blessings and healing for those areas of our lives that may have been traumatised. It also helps us to keep things in balance because no matter how difficult things may be at the moment, with Jesus there is hope for a brighter future. The Lord also helps us with our successes, as He brings balance and enable us to go forward in His perfect will. Whatever the purpose that God has for us, we are assured of His presence with us each step of the way.

A short prayer.

Father we come into your presence and are grateful that you have a plan for our lives and that you never leave us or forsake us but are there for us. We ask that regardless of what we have experienced we give all our joys and all our troubles to you. We ask for your forgiveness for the times you have answered our prayers and we have failed to acknowledge you, we also ask forgiveness for the times we have failed to spend times with you or have taken your blessings for granted. We come to you because we want to change and to develop our relationship with you. We invite you back into our lives and we ask that you help us to spend quality time with you as we develop our friendship and relationship with you in Jesus name we pray, Amen

3

BE HOLY AS I AM HOLY

In search of excellence

Years and years ago I wanted to be a track and field athlete, it was my main goal and objective for life. I joined an athletics club and I trained three sometimes four times a week with the club and went out for training runs virtually every day. I was a middle distance athlete and ran 800 and 1500 metres, I also ran cross-country for the same athletic club and I had a dream of making it into the Great Britain team some day and going to the Olympics. Each year I improved and my personal best times got better each year, but in truth I was never good enough to run for my country or to make it to the Olympics. It did however make me appreciate what it takes to be a world class athlete and the dedication and the ability needed to be an Olympic or world champion. Athletes strive in all weathers to be champions and yet there can only be one champion at each distance in any given year.

My competitiveness in track and field was carried over into all aspects of my adult life, in as much as, in everything I did I wanted to do my absolute best. I strived to improve and be better each day and was driven onwards all the time to be the very best that I could be. However, I found out very quickly that I wasn't perfect and that perfection was something that was beyond my grasp. This has been a hindrance and a difficulty for me all my adult life. How do we accept that we are not perfect and we make mistakes and get things wrong from time-to-time? Especially in a world that is unforgiving and in a career that for many demands perfection and frowns on mistakes almost as if they are some form of heinous crime.

If we cannot measure up to the demands made upon us by mankind, how can we measure up to what God demands of us?

Being Holy

What does it mean to be holy? How do we begin to define holiness? It would take a whole book by itself to define holiness and even the dictionaries struggle to define holiness (see Baker's Evangelical Dictionary of Biblical Theology[1]). The short definition is that holiness and to be holy is what God is.[1] Therefore when God calls us to be holy as He is holy[2] He is calling us to be like Him. We can see from the dictionary, that holiness includes being set apart, being pure without defect and has connotations of being perfect.[1]

From the Bible we know there are three levels to being holy. Some versions of the Bible calls it sanctification, a word meaning being set apart for God.[1] The three area to being holy are; firstly, we are holy when we confess Jesus as Lord and saviour and accept Him[3], this is positional sanctification. Jesus then has freed us from a life of slavery to sin and we should cherish our position of being made right with our heavenly Father.[4] We can also have confidence of who we are, and our new position in Christ going forward because of the promises that Jesus has made to us.[5] These are promises that confirm our position in Christ, that we are made right with God through our relationship with Jesus. Part of our position in Jesus is that we don't face God's anger and have been released from our past into the promise of new things in Christ.[6] In a nutshell we are holy because God says we are holy. The second area of holiness is progressive holiness, as we live on this earth we are becoming more holy as we grow in faith and understanding. The third area of holiness is complete holiness when we meet the Lord we will be like him.

Hindrances to holiness

Most people have skeletons in their closet and have done things they are not proud of or have taken actions that are positively evil in the sight of the Lord. Sometimes people will justify their actions, such as 'well that person really deserved it', or 'someone had to get involved and sort the person out'. Probably the most common excuse we use when we have done something that we know is wrong and against our position in Jesus, is to deny it or hide it away hoping nobody will find out, some people even go as far as confessing openly that they have done nothing wrong at all. Sin can hide the crime and in our guilt we deceive ourselves and often others to the true nature of the sin we have committed.

Indeed, the Apostle Paul declared that like all men he found himself doing things that he really shouldn't be doing and he hated doing, things that were sinful and against God.[7] Nothing good can come from our sinful nature and even though we desperately desire to do well, we are incapable of bringing that into being in our own strength.[7] For those who desire to move forward with the Lord, there is a daily struggle against the ways of the flesh and the sin that comes naturally to what the Bible calls the carnal man.[7] We struggle with all kinds of lusts and potential pitfalls and many seek to escape the old way of life and live for Jesus.

God is gracious with our struggles and the Holy Spirit within us enables us to overcome the temptations that would draw us back into darkness. Therefore, what does it mean that we are not condemned?[6] It means exactly what it says. If we sin then we have the option to continue sinning, and re-entering into darkness, or coming before the Lord and confessing our sin and asking for His forgiveness.

Be sure sin leads to death[8] and the concept of God's judgment on a wicked world is not a popular topic amongst many modern theologians but it is a clear teaching in the Bible. The good news is that we have crossed over from darkness into His light the moment we accept Jesus as our Lord and Saviour and confess our need to be saved.[5]

The moment we accept Jesus as Lord and Saviour we start a journey with God. The goal of that journey is to transform us from what we were into the likeness of Jesus. Being Holy as God is Holy[2] is all about gradually changing into the likeness of Jesus.

Progressive holiness

If the first part to being holy is that God says that we are holy then the second part is progressive holiness, which can be defined as becoming holy in an ongoing process throughout the course of our lives. The intention is that we strive to become more like Jesus every day, a process that will last our entire lives. Progressive sanctification is something we all struggle with as we try to follow God's ways in our daily lives. If we love Jesus we will do everything we can to do His will, and to follow His ways, and to become more and more like Him.[9] We are going forward with God. Progressive sanctification is supported by the truth of what God has started He will finish.[10]

We are work in progress and although at times we struggle with sin and feel anything but clean, our Holy Father is working in us to complete the good work He began the day we accepted Jesus as our Lord and Saviour. Our heavenly Father hasn't given up on us, we are not yet the finished product, and we still have many flaws and things in our characters that God wants to change. He will continue to change us and like a patient potter with a prized pot, He will form and shape us and continue to work on us as a craftsman works until He has satisfied that we are complete, that we are like Him, and the end product will be a work of art, something extremely beautiful.

This is why we face difficulties, because through hardship, the chips and impurities, the flaws and the imperfections that need to come out of our character are slowly but surely knocked away. Be encouraged by the difficult times because God is working so we will become like Him. So rejoice and be glad because God is at work. Some of us are big projects and it's like going onto a building site where the sign 'Beware men working overhead' or 'Everyone must wear a hard hat when entering this site' is displayed. Only with God the sign is 'God is working on our heads and minds to get our thinking and our attitudes to be like His'. God hasn't given up, He is only just beginning and the work will continue until we are called up to heaven then we will be like Him.

The final part of that journey will be when we finally join up with Jesus, and we will then be just like Him and then the journey will be complete.[11] This is called complete holiness or complete sanctification. We will have completed God's desire that we are holy like Him. God's purpose for us is to make us more like Jesus in our attitudes, our beliefs and our deepest thoughts and desires. God wants to remove from our lives the worldly things that so hinder our walk with Him and there are so many of them.

What are the dangers?

There are many warnings in the Bible to live our lives in God's ways according to the Spirit and not in the way of the world. The warnings include not continuing to live our old life and not to continue with all the bad habits that God set us free from.[12] The Bible goes even further and provides us with a list of acts and attitudes that are against God's way.[13]

Sexual immorality and fornication is often or nearly always placed at the top of the list of Biblical warnings for good reason.[13] Sexual immorality is simply having sex with another person we are not married too. The sexual drive in both men and women is one of the strongest natural desires, and in Western society it is impossible to open our eyes without potentially being faced with sexual images. Sex in its crudest forms is used to sell just about anything from cars, razor blades, clothes, beauty products, cosmetics, toothpaste, etc. The world is obsessed with sex and most popular television programmes use sexual attraction as a subplot to capture and keep our attention. God intended sex as the ultimate human intimacy between a husband and wife within the confines of marriage.[14] Yet the world has turned sex into an industry and has sold it as a right for all whether we are married or not.

There is another reason why sexual immorality is at the top of the list and that is because it is one of the few sins that affects our body.[15] All other sins occur outside the body but sexual sin occurs within our body therefore it is more important than many other sins. However sin is sin and to commit one sin makes it easier to justify when committing other sins.

The principal here is that when we become a Christian Jesus came into our hearts so that God lives within us.[9] God is an intimate part of us, and therefore, sexual sin is allowing our body that should be a temple for God become something that is abhorrent and evil in His sight. Satan uses this temptation against Christians, and particularly against Christian leaders, to great success, and there have been sadly a number of high profile cases in recent years where powerful Christian men and women with strong Spirit filled ministries have fallen for this temptation and have lost their ministries. Brothers and sisters' guard our hearts against such thoughts and actions because sexual immorality and sexual temptation is the biggest and most deadly weapon Satan uses against us. The hurt and devastation that this sin causes is immense, not just for perpetrators and the person they sin with, but for both sets of families including unsuspecting spouses and the children of these families. Flee sexual immorality do not allow it to take a foothold in our hearts.

One of the biggest tricks of Satan when using sexual immorality is that of justifying the sin in the believer's heart. Do not be deceived, those who commit sexual immorality without repentance will not enter the Kingdom of God.[16] Yet even for those who have fallen into this sin God has a way back to salvation but it is a long and painful road.

Idolatry often accompanies sexual immorality and idolatry can be defined as anything that takes the place of God in our lives.[17] Idolatry can come in many disguises, such as our career, our home, our children, our sports interests, for example, if we support a football or soccer team, baseball or basketball or ice hockey team and that becomes more important to us than serving God, then we should be concerned that an idol may be lurking in our hearts. Our appearance and the way we look can become an idol if we are constantly thinking about it at the exclusion of all other things. This can be a particular problem especially among teenagers and women of all ages. Just look at how much is spent on advertising beauty products.

Money is often an idol in the lives of men or women and I feel concerned when I hear a verse often quoted by rich people "it's not money that is the root of sin but the love of money."[18] People who quote that verse usually have a problem with money which they seek to justify in their own eyes and in the eyes of others. Don't be fooled, God will not be mocked and the biggest hindrances to our walk with God is the sins we justify in our own eyes and hearts. If we spend more time thinking about money or a sports team or our children or anything else than we think about more than thinking about the Lord then we may have a problem with idolatry. If we are unsure if that is the case and we genuinely want to know, then simply sit down quietly with God and ask Him to show us if there is anything in our hearts that is coming before Him and if there is God will show us. Then we can repent of that sin and move forward on our journey with the Lord. God has promised that He will set us free from the things that bind us and hold us back from being the person that He desires us to be.

For those of us that are concerned and worried about sins in our life or feel bound by some spirit of idolatry and are seeking deliverance, may I suggest prayerfully reading Psalm 107 which is helpful for addressing our concerns.

Rivalry is another problem for Christians in the Western World which is often disguised as a need to be successful or a continual striving to climb up the career ladder. It is a particular problem for Christians living in the Western World were success is often seen as God's blessing on our lives. As I stated earlier television evangelists may inform their listeners that God wants to make them financially rich. Another concern is those that claim to have God's secret for our success and for a small donation will send us a book unlocking these secrets. However it is probably wise to remember that these books do not take into consideration God's plan for our lives and there may be a very good reason why God has us in a job that we may not necessarily enjoy, or why at this moment in our lives we are struggling financially and so forth, God may simply want to teach us to trust and depend upon Him for our needs at this moment in time. If we are struggling right now take heart because the Lord is teaching us something special that is vitally important for our walk with Him and for our future in His Kingdom.

Difficulties and trials

Whatever difficulties and trials we may encounter, they are only temporary. When we successfully come out the other side, we will have grown in the Lord and have taken an important step on the journey to being more Christ like. Believe me when I say do not disregard the difficult times because they are the most important for our relationship with God and our journey to becoming Holy as God is Holy.

There will be a time when we have come through our trial and look back at what the Lord has taught us and how He has changed us. Ultimately, the Lord wants us to grow and He wants to bless us through that growing experience.[19]

The blessings of the Lord

Once we have accepted Jesus as our Saviour, there are no catches to the Lord's blessing. They are not conditional on anything we have to do or achieve. Don't be mistaken into thinking that blessings from God are merely financial or a plan to make us rich. In my experience the Lord is far more concerned with the state of our hearts than whether or not we have financial wealth. There is far more to life than the accumulation of wealth and possessions, such as, how we interact with the people around us, our attitude toward those who need help or are weak and poor. Blessings can come in many shapes and forms, such as the beautiful world we live in, a beautiful sunset or sunrise, or seeing some great valley or mountains for the very first time reminds us of the awesome power and great creative ability of God. We can be greatly blessed by a small gift from a friend or from a family member or a kind word or a loving hug. When we take time to think about the wonderful things that God has already done for our lives then we can see the rich blessings we have received from His hand. The truly exciting thing is that there are many more blessings to come in the future. The possibilities are endless and unlimited with God.

Paul learnt this lesson more than most because he knew what it was like to be in need and also knew what it was like to be rich. The secret is to be content in every situation.[20] The world is always striving after the next step on the way to success. People in the world seek to have a bit more money than they have already, to have a bigger car or a bigger house than the one they possess. To treat themselves so they are more attractive or more successful than they are now, until chasing after worldly possessions and beauty becomes an obsession that can never be satisfied. We as Christians have been called to be different, to be set apart, to be identified by their love for one another, and God and not for their love of worldly possessions.

> *We need to be content regardless of our circumstances. Let go and let God take care of our circumstances.*

Being content in God is exactly where the Lord wants us to be, ever trusting in Him and in the power of His might. We have discussed the negative influence of the world and we return to discuss where God is leading us in His walk with us through our day to day lives.

What God has begun in us He will finish. God does not give up once He starts a project and sometimes His work in people's lives is difficult to identify.[21] Something that starts out as an inanimate object can through great workmanship turned into a vessel so beautiful that it takes our breath away. When the Lord has finished working in us, and with us, then we will be transformed into someone who is beautiful in every way. The beauty the Lord offers is a transformed life of inner beauty that reflects His likeness in every way.

The word of God tells us what it is like when we surrender and allow God to work through His Spirit in our lives.[22] We are changed, our perspective on life changes, we become content and we start to show the traits and attitudes that tells us that God is working in us. Have we ever had someone tell us that we've changed that there is something different about us? Has a non-Christian told us that there is something different about us that they just can't figure out? Then the Lord is working in our lives and the fruit is growing.

Love is the greatest part of being a Christian.[23] God places love above everything, without love we are nothing, yet it is the most difficult for us to do on so many fronts.[23] The people who hurt us the most are the ones we love the most. To truly love with everything we have is what God commands, and what He expects from us yet we so often fall short of these standards. When the Bible talks about our hearts it's not referring to the physical organ but to the effective centre of our being. Our inner most selves. At the centre of our being should be love for God and for our fellow humans. The love that the God asks for is unconditional, not reserved not holding back but fully committed.

Biblical love is a love that passes all understanding. It is the type of love that knows no limits and one which makes sacrifices. Truly loving parents will make any sacrifice for their children, some parents even lay down their lives for their children. That is the kind of love that God commands from His children that we love Him sacrificially. To make sure that God has the greatest place in our lives, that He fills our inner most being. God loves us deeply and He asks that we do the same for Him

This is the highest calling of man, to love the Lord God with all our souls and all our minds and all our hearts and in this context soul probably refers to our lives.[23] God is looking for us to live our lives in a manner that reveals our love for Him. The truly great men of God throughout history have been able to reach this highest echelon of being able to live their lives truly 100% committed to God, and God has been able to bless them in a manner few of us ever experience. To reach that level of love toward God means that we are in constant contact with the living God where every breath that we take is filled with love for God. There is great joy and great contentment to reach that level of relationship with God, there are no words to describe the feeling of being truly in love with

God in our inner most being and in everything we do in our lives.

> **The greatest form of worship is to love the Lord our God with all our hearts and all our minds and all our souls.**[23]

The highest form of worship, however, is the love the Lord our God with all of our minds.[23] To get to the position where everything that enters our minds and leaves them is full of the love of God. In the modern world with its great demands is it possible to love the Lord your God with all of our minds? Yes, it is!! Without a doubt it is possible to fill our minds with the love of God. To make every response to every question, to every thought, to every reaction and response to whatever life is sending our way a response of the love of God. Whatever comes our way we can choose to respond with the love of God. It is not easy and indeed without God it is impossible.[24] We can through prayer and by filling our minds with the word of God reach a level where our minds and souls are filled with the love of God.

So much of our response to our everyday situations starts in our mind. How do we respond when we are disappointed? How do we respond when people hurt us, or abuse us, or let us down? How do we respond when God does not answer our deepest prayers or the answer is no? If we can respond with love for God then we will grow spiritually to be the person God wants us to be and to achieve that goal is the greatest blessing we can ever imagine. Truly brothers and sisters to love God with all our inner most being, all of our lives and with everything within our minds and souls is truly wonderful and marvellous and something near understanding what the Kingdom of God is truly like. The Bible tells us that the Kingdom of God is precious and valuable.[25]

> **Finding the Kingdom of God is like finding the greatest treasure of all, it surpasses everything else in all the world.[25]**

Finding God is like finding the greatest treasure that we will ever have, it surpasses everything else imaginable.[25] Is knowing God so wonderful and that His love fills us so much that we treasure it above all else? When we truly love like that then we have found the fulfilment that the Bible talks so much about. A love that is so great it cannot be described in words. One day we will meet our Saviour and we will experience that great love and deep fulfilment that can only come through being united with the living God.[26] That is our calling and that is our destiny. We may never quite reach those heights on earth but when we think about the descriptions of worship in the book of Revelation.[26] We will certainly reach the indescribable heights of loving the Lord our God with all of our hearts and minds and souls in heaven.

When we achieve that level of love for God then we will be very close to being holy as God is holy.[2] God's purpose for each one of us is that we learn to love Him as He loves us. Unreservedly, unconditionally, not holding anything back. Our love for Him should come before anything else in our lives and that is the greatest challenge facing Christians in the Western World today. We have lost the great love for God. We have mostly stopped loving God for who He is and we focus like little babies only on what we get from Him. Give me, give me, give me has become our every prayer and our every desire.

Our prayer should be Lord help us delight ourselves in You and please fill our hearts with Your desires not ours, may Yours goals be our goals and may we seek more and more to be like You in every way possible.[27]

> **Beloved we can trust God in all things for in the end things will work out in favour of the righteous.**

A short prayer.

Father teach us to love you with all of our hearts, all of our souls and all of our minds. Thank you we can obtain that level of love while living here on earth. Lord make our every desire your desire and our every thought your thoughts. Fill us to over flowing with your unconditional love. Refocus our lives so they are more like that of your Son and our Lord Jesus. Thank you that you so loved us that you gave your one and only Son and whoever believes in Him will have eternal life. But thank you more than everything that you who began a good work in us will carry it on to completion. Amen

4

THE FRUIT OF THE SPIRIT

Buying fruit

We all have our favourite food and meals we love to eat. We probably have our favourite fruit and the great thing about fruit is that it comes in many different varieties. From time to time may come across a fruit that we have never seen or even heard of before. We may even have to go to some exotic destination to find such fruit. My favourite experience of eating fruit came several years ago when I was fortunate enough to travel to Cabo, San Lucas in Mexico which is on the Pacific coast. From London, England it takes about 24 hours to reach Cabo. As I had breakfast sitting on the veranda watching the whales and dolphins, it was the taste of the fresh pineapples that made the trip memorable as it was by far the most delicious fruit I'd ever tasted. I still haven't worked out quite what made the pineapples taste so different but they were more refreshing and appetising than any pineapples I had eaten before or eaten since.

The taste lingers on even today, but I wonder if I returned to Cabo would the pineapples still taste the same? Was it merely the moment, and experience of seeing the Pacific Ocean for the first time, sitting on the veranda in the warm sunshine to eat breakfast that made the taste so unique or were the pineapples exactly as I remember them absolutely delicious?

The thing about fruit is that it needs to be continually replenished, once a tree has yielded its harvest of pineapples it needs to regrow some more. Fruit is a great gift from God and is packed with all sorts of essential ingredients that are needed to keep our bodies healthy and free from disease.[1] By the same margin and criteria when the Bible talks about the fruit of the Spirit it must also be vital for our spiritual welfare and growth.[2]

What does it mean to love?

We have already discussed what love is and that we are being transformed to be holy like God. So perhaps it's not surprising to see that the first fruit of the Spirit is love.[2] We are called to love, it is the most important component to our being, we exist to love and to be loved.[3] The love God is looking for in our lives needs to transcend and rise above our prejudices. It needs to move above our earthly desires and we need to love those who are unlovable. Within our lives God allows someone, somewhere, at some point in time, who we just cannot get along with no matter how hard we try, and that person is like a piece of sandpaper constantly rubbing the rough edges of our lives away. Whether at work, or at church, there will be someone, somewhere who just rubs us up the wrong way. Those are the people that God has sent to test whether we truly have His love in our hearts for our neighbours.

> **Love is at the centre of everything.**
> **Without love, everything we accomplish**
> **lacks meaning and purpose.**[4]

Our greatest challenge in our walk with God is to desire to love others as God loves them, and to desire that fruit in our life above other fruits of the Spirit.

In recent years, Christians in many denominations have focused on acquiring the gifts of the Spirit, and among some Christian's and denominations speaking in tongues has become a necessity, and a gift so valued that in some quarters it stands above all other heavenly gifts at the expense of others. Indeed I remember entering a church back in the 1970s and being asked even before they found out my name if I spoke in tongues as this was a test of whether or not I was a true believer. Yet the fruit of the Spirit is what should separate Christians from the world and again love is top of the list.

When the Apostle Paul turned to discuss what is important in the Christian life he began with love. He distinguished it from speaking in tongues, from prophecy, and from other gifts.[4] Paul felt the necessity to put the record straight and tell us that without love we are nothing. Even in the early church, it was the gifts of the Spirit that men and women most coveted above the fruit of the Spirit.[4] However, Jesus last discussion with His disciples before going to the cross centred on bearing fruit.[5] Indeed, Jesus taught that God would cut off every branch that did not bear fruit and would tend those branches who desired to bear fruit so that they would become even more fruitful. In the same passage Jesus also talked about the love He had for those who believe and He expected believers to remain in His love. We have discussed God's love for us and defined love in the first chapter of this book, we now return to consider love as a fruit of our lives.

What men and women aim for in life is so often wide of the mark of what God thinks is important. We look for things that make us look good to others and that give us a platform for others to admire us. In other words we want to be worshipped like God. However, without love we are wide of the mark and we have nothing.[4] The fact about love is that we are born with it, but then our experiences of life will either enhance the love we have or will prejudice it and cause it to fade and die. We may be confused by what love is, but the Bible tells exactly what love is so that we needn't fret and worry about understanding it.[6] Love isn't some gooey sentiment, love requires action and it requires action from us.

Love is doing something good for people who don't deserve it, we can choose to love people by saying something kind instead of using unkind words. Sometimes we really have to try hard and love even when we don't feel like it. How does love relate to fruit? As we have seen fruit is available in season, there is a time and place when we can buy certain fruit because it harvest time for that particular fruit. However, the fruit of the Spirit should be evident all year round and should be a natural extension of who we are. How do we react when someone says something nasty about us or is just plain cruel toward us, do we react in love? It is not easy to respond in love, to pray for that person or to even help that person when they are sad and hurting. We cultivate the fruit in our lives by watering it in prayer, we ask God to fill us with more love, especially for our enemies and the people we don't particularly like.

Expressions of love

We all long to be treated with patience and kindness and how refreshing it is to find people who don't insist on having their own way. It is something beautiful to see two young people truly in love when everything is pure and their beloved is the apple of their eyes. It is even more beautiful to see people who have been together for decades still in love and totally enthralled with each other. To find someone to love us in this way is a deep longing for each one of us and the depth of our need for love is amazing. We long for someone to love us with a deep passion and caring, someone who looks at us with all our faults yet still loves us. That is the love that God has for us. To love us just as we are but God also sees the people we can become and our true potential and works in our lives to gently move us onto a new level in our development and walk with Him.

Overcoming hurt to gain the blessing

God's love for us is amazing but many of us fail to experience His love either because of our childhood experiences which have damaged us or because we are simply too busy and stressed with everyday lives to stop and receive His love. Like all relationships it takes time for it to develop and make it stronger and for us to be able to experience God's love for us, flowing out from His throne of grace. We need to enter our prayer closets, where we can be still and quiet in God's presence, and then ask for His love to fill us and heal us in our mind and souls.

However, there are many blockages that prevent us receiving God's love. For example, our past experiences that has left us feeling inadequate or not worthy to be loved or even worst we believe we are unlovable. If there is anything that is preventing us from receiving all of God's love then we need to lift that up to the Lord and ask Him for healing. Also ask Him to help us to forgive the person who has caused us that great pain because forgiveness is central to us being able to receive God's love. If we need to forgive ourselves for something we have done wrong then also we should take time to pray for this too.

Being able to receive love and being healed from past hurts is important because we are called to love others as we love ourselves.[7] The first step in being able to love others as ourselves is to receive God's love in our hearts and our innermost beings because that is often where we have been hurt the most.

The second step in being able to love others as we love ourselves is to truly love ourselves. It seems the simplest thing but often loving ourselves is difficult. I am shocked by the number of people out there that find it difficult to love themselves. Often people have done something bad in the past and find it difficult to forgive themselves for their action. The longer that time has passed the harder it is to forgive ourselves and the sin builds itself into a stronghold in our lives preventing us from receiving love and from loving ourselves. We need to tear down this stronghold and flatten it in order to allow the Holy Spirit to come in and fill us with the love of God and to enable ourselves to love who we are.

Brothers and sisters we often fret that we have committed the unforgiveable sin when we haven't or have done something so bad that we cannot be forgiven. Self-forgiveness is vitally important to enable us to receive the love of God and to be able to love ourselves.

The unforgiveable sin is blasphemy against the Holy Spirit[8] and is committed by those who reject Jesus as Lord and Saviour and go further than that in calling the works of the Holy Spirit as coming from Satan.[8] People who do such things already hate God and reject everything that is Christian. True believers have never done such things even those who have grown up in pagan or unbelieving families.

The bigger problem is self-forgiveness for sins we may have committed against others and our actions often carried out in temper that have deeply hurt others. There is no sin so deep that God cannot reach us and heal us however terrible the sin if we are willing to place that sin in the hands of God.[9] We will find that God has already forgiven us and what we really need to do is to forgive ourselves and move on. Now is the time for us to receive that forgiveness. Quietly lift that up to the Lord and wait to receive His peace. Sometimes it takes time but if when we have lifted the problem to God then His peace will surely come.

The final step is loving others as ourselves is to just go and do it. Be sure that God bless us as we move forward in this way.

Joy

The second fruit of the Spirit is the joy of the Lord.[2] Joy comes out of receiving God's love and out of loving ourselves. The true joy of release and falling back in love with God is immense. There is a great strength that comes out of being filled with joy.[10] There is something infectious about being around a joyous person, they are able to change our mood and challenge us about how we are feeling.

> **Our strength and victory comes from the joy we have in the Lord.[10]**

Failure to love ourselves really is to place ourselves in grief but the release we get from loving ourselves allows us to live in real joy and there is a great strength living in the joy that comes from knowing God.[10] We are missing a great deal in life because we have moved so far away from what is important. We need to find the intense love for God so that out of that relationship we can truly be filled with joy.[11]

We lack joy because we haven't asked God to fill us with His joy, but also because we haven't grasped who we are in Christ. Do we really understand what we have received by becoming Christians? Do we take for granted our position in Christ without really appreciating the wonder and awe of what God has done for us?

Start the day with joy and then joy will be with us throughout the day.[12] Be truly grateful for all that the Lord has done for us in bringing us this far. Joy is a wonderful fruit of the Spirit that is often overlooked. Joy comes out of an appreciation of what the Lord Jesus has truly done for us and is an essential part of our overcoming the world. Do we appreciate the depth of sacrifice that Jesus gave on the cross at Calvary? Do we appreciate where we were on the way to a godless eternity before Christ found us?

The real blockage to us experiencing the joy of the Lord is a familiarity that we find especially in Western Christianity where we simply take everything for granted. Stop for a moment and ask yourself when the last time you experienced joy in your heart? Do you have joy in your heart there right now? Then think of three things that the Lord has done for you that should make you joyful. Hold onto those thoughts and allow the joy to flow through your hearts. We as Christians need to go and find the joy of the Lord because it has largely gone from the church. In the coming dark days we will need the joy of the Lord to bring light to the darkness, to overcome and cast it out. It is essential that we recognise and reclaim the joy of the Lord. It can be a real challenge to maintain joy when we face trials and tribulations but the challenges of life come from God in order to strengthen our faith and our perseverance. This is so that we can become mature children of God.[13]

Facing trials is not the thing that immediately comes to mind when we consider joy but the Bible teaches us that trials are part of our education as we grow from little children into mature Christian adults.[13] The trials that we face will either bring us closer to God or drive us further away. The choice is ours and how we respond to trials says a lot about our love for God and where we are on the road to heaven.

Often we miss out on the blessings of God because we don't ask and we don't stand on the promises in the Bible.[14] Ask so that your joy may be complete.[14]

Lord give me patience and I want it now

It always intrigues me the order of the fruit of the Spirit particularly in this fast moving world of ours where everything is instantaneous. The third fruit of the Spirit is patience[2] and may be because when we are seeking the love and joy of the Lord then we have to be patient before we receive the answers to our prayers.

> **Trials come to test whether our joy is truly founded on God and in order for us to grow in our faith. God desires that we have the fullest of joy.[14]**

I have heard on occasion people pray for something and almost demand that the Lord provides immediately. Lord I would like you to give me patience and I want it now. When I was a young Christian at University in England I remember praying for patience because I wasn't at all patient, in fact I was very impatient. I prayed for days for the Lord to give me more patience and the irony of it I couldn't understand why God was not answering. My prayers for patience went from being days into weeks then into months and then even into years yet I still had no outward sign that anything had happened. The one day it dawned on me I had been praying for more patience for 3 years and during that time I patiently waited for the Lord to answer that prayer in full expectation of an instantaneous answer. Some 35 years later one of my colleagues at work recently remarked that she loved working with me because I was the most patient person she had ever met. Sometimes God's answers to our prayers are not conceivable or real to us but He does answer prayer. It also takes time to develop patience.

Listening to young people today they cannot imagine a world without the internet or mobile phones. What did people do before they were able to send text messages? My earthly father was a seaman and was away for 11 months of the year and I remember as a small boy writing an airmail letter to him when he was working on a world cruise. It was 6 weeks before we received a reply. Patience is a virtue but we have become accustomed to instant everything. Microwaveable meals instead of good old fashion cooking that our Grandma's used to cook. Yet we forget the former way of life. So patience no longer comes naturally. We need patience to ensure that we can keep going in times of difficulties.[15]

When we are facing difficulties then we need to be patient and wait for the Lord to lead us through the storm into the safe haven. It is difficult to wait when things around us are stormy or if we see a deadline approaching and we feel we have to respond.

Waiting for the Lord is a valuable and important attribute for every Christian and in the turbulent world we live in patience is required more and more. Being patient will have a great reward in itself on this earth, but is a vital fruit if we are to be obedient to the Lord, and most of all if we are to receive God's best for our lives.

Why is patience and waiting important? God often tests us to see if we really trust Him and sometimes that means putting us in situations where we have to wait for an answer to our prayers. Waiting is vital if we are asking God to show us if it is the right thing to do for example should we accept the offer of a new job or when choosing a life partner. We wait for the Lord to answer our prayers or to provide guidance and the temptation is press forward without Him often with disastrous consequences. Wait for the Lord. Apart from obedience, patience and waiting on the Lord is the only way to obtain God's best for our lives. What seems good to us may not be what is best for us and therefore to wait is invaluable. Another reason for patience is that it renews us and strengthens our walk with the Lord.[16]

> **Take time out from the battle to rest and wait upon the Lord so that we can renew our strength.**[16]

Waiting for the Lord renews our strength for the battle and takes us to new heights in our relationship with the living God.[16] The Lord teaches us so much during the waiting time that it is worth every second.

Waiting on the Lord comes down to how much we really trust Him. It is also a good time for the dark hidden secrets of our hearts to be revealed, so they can be dealt with as we continue our walk with God. We find ourselves questioning the Lord, does He really care? Is He going to answer my prayer? Will He meet my need? Will He change my circumstances? That is why we need to know the Bible, to know that God does have plans for us, good and rewarding plans for the future. Trust in the Lord. These times of patient waiting are designed to give us perseverance and increase our faith.

The power of kindness

Kindness comes out of patience and it is a wonderful fruit to possess.[2] Sometimes all the kindness required is to be sensitive and receptive to the people God sends our way. Kind words can change people and can transform situations from being tense and strained into becoming happy and light hearted and jovial. Do not under estimate the power of words or the lasting impact they have on others.

Kindness stretches beyond just words and acts of kindness especially when given to those who cannot repay the kindness will have an eternal impact on many. I would encourage us wherever possible to develop the fruit of kindness because it will help the Kingdom of heaven grow more than we can imagine.

Being kind and doing good deeds are part of the makeup of every believer in Christ. Let us never give up on seeking opportunities to be kind and to carry out good acts in the name of the Lord.

Sometimes good deeds come at a cost as anyone who has read the story of Corrie Ten Boom, whose family helped the Jewish people escape the Nazi oppression in the Netherlands during the Second World War.[18] can testify. Ultimately they paid a very high price for their acts of kindness with both the father and her sister dying. Corrie spent several years in a concentration camp for her family's kindness to the Jewish people fleeing for their lives. Kindness and goodness go together as fruits of the Spirit.

Faithfulness a rarity in the world

Faithfulness is fast becoming a rarity in the world we live in. In sport we see professional sports clubs drop players because they are too old, or because they haven't performed to the required standard over a specified period, or they are injured, or simply because there is someone better, fitter or faster out there. On the other hand we see sportsmen and women who are the stars of their particular clubs moving on because they want more success or they can get more money elsewhere. Likewise in the workplace people are made redundant because they are no longer needed, or are surplus to requirements, or are not in the plans of a new boss even though they may be vastly experienced and have been with a company for many years. Also more and more spouses are becoming unfaithful and in a recent survey 44% of people admitted being unfaithful to their partners.[19]

Being faithful is the next fruit of the Spirit and as with all the other fruit, it is an important characteristic that separates us as Christians from the world.[2] Beloved, faithfulness may come at a great price,[20] but know this the Lord will preserve the faithful and will give each one a crown of life.[21]

Faithfulness is important to the Lord and can come at a considerable cost but hold on to your faith in every situation and God will provide for you. It may not be easy to hold onto faith as the days of darkness draw near, and remaining faithful to the Lord is going to become more difficult for those who truly believe in Christ.

As Christians, remaining faithful to the Lord may take many different forms, for example, it may mean continuing to be a witness for the Lord in our workplace among the few or no other Christians in the office. Remaining to stand for Christian values when the temptation is to remain quiet. Remember faithfulness is rewarded with the crown of life.[20] Standing up for the Lord will not make us popular among the worldly minded, but it will make our light shine and God will be faithful to you if we are faithful to Him. Also no matter how many times we may have failed in the past, new beginnings are a gift from God and tomorrow may provide the opportunity to put things right.[20] Never give up hope. Never dwell on past failings, always look forward to the next opportunity and challenge.

Gentleness

In the harsh world we live, in gentleness is an attribute that is clearly in short supply. Patients in the UK have complained about the rudeness of staff and the lack of compassion.[23] Indeed the Nursing Times devoted an entire supplement on the need for compassionate nursing in 2011.[24] The supplement outlines the history of compassionate nursing which can be traced to the Christian morality brought to nursing by Florence Nightingale.[25] The main traits of gentleness include but are not limited to, compassion, kindness, sympathy, sensitivity to a person's situation and empathy which is an ability to identify with the sufferer and understand what they are going through.[26]

John R. Clarke

In Europe we face the influx of hundreds of thousands of refugees fleeing from war and oppressive regimes in North Africa. Thousands upon thousands are paying everything they have to get to Europe for a better life, literally thousands of men, women and children have drowned trying to escape the oppression.[27] European Governments don't know how to respond to the situation and debate on how the deter these desperate people from coming.[28] Where oh Lord is the compassion and empathy for people who are fleeing for their lives and I wonder how the people who make these decisions would feel if the boot was on the other foot and they were fleeing for their lives? The world desperately needs Christian compassion and gentleness and care.[29] We were asked by Jesus shortly before He returned to His Father in heaven to go and make disciples throughout the world.[30] However, as far as Europe is concerned God is sending the world to us through the growing number of refugees fleeing from terror in their own countries.

> *In your hearts honour Jesus and don't quarrel but respond to every challenge with respect and compassion.*

What a difference it would make to the world if there were many more people who were able to show gentleness and compassion in the dealings with others. Let us be filled with His Spirit to the level that gentleness flows from us.[2] The fruit of the Spirit like any fruit on a tree will grow as we grow in the Lord and we are all work in progress. God is gracious to give us whatever we ask for in prayer and for the fruit of the Spirit to be more evident in us, is a wonderful place to start our prayers.[2]

Self-control

Self-control is the last fruit of the Spirit listed in Galatians but it is by no means the least.[2] There are many things in life that provoke us to anger but the Bible pleads with us to show self-control and restraint.[31] Sometimes that can be very difficult but anger especially unrighteous anger does great harm to others and it is with good cause that the fruit of the Spirit is self-control. Anger can be very destructive while self-control can provide a balm that defuses potentially explosive situations. Let us be a people that bring healing to those who are hurting.

A short prayer

Father when we study the fruit of the Spirit we are convicted of our failings and shortcomings therefore we ask that you will gently change us to be filled with more fruit of your Spirit as we grow in you. Thank you for the progress we have made in our walk with you so far and thank you that there is so much more that we can experience if we make you the centre of our daily lives. Remind us daily of who we are and fill us each day with more fruit as the Holy Spirit comes into our lives and revives us. We ask in our precious Lord Jesus name, Amen.

5

CHRIST HAS SET YOU FREE

Being set free

It is a terrible thing to be locked up and unable to have the freedom to go where you want to go. There are lots of different ways to be imprisoned apart from the obvious of thieves, criminals and offenders who are locked away for crimes. Some people are house bound and unable to leave their homes either through illness or through old age or a fear of open spaces. Others may be locked in a dysfunctional body. Even in the modern age there are some people who are trapped in slavery, or a dead end job, or an abusive relationship. Some people long to escape from oppressive Governments to a better and more secure life. Still others will want to be set free from an unhealthy addictions or habits. Whatever the reason for being trapped, most people long to be set free. Although some people may have given up hope that they will ever be set free, the Bible offers hope for those who have a longing to be set free.[1]

What happens when people are set free or escape from whatever is binding them? There are number of emotions that they might experience, for some this might be a sense of overwhelming relief and euphoria in finally being set free. For Christians being set free brings us much closer to God as we depend upon Him for our freedom. With freedom comes the victory to finally overcome whatever has held us back and prevented us from moving forward.

On our journey

Staying free is another matter as there is sometimes the temptation to return to the former life that held us in captivity for so long. If a repetitive sin was the issue that bound us then there might be a temptation to return to that sin. If it was some other kind of slavery that held us captive, then we might want to return to the old life because of the security it offered even though we know it was wrong. In fact the old life of captivity for some may seem attractive compared to the insecurity that freedom sometimes appears to give.

Freedom will remain for as long as we stay focused on the Lord and trust Him to lead us away from temptation into the new found freedom that He provides. We must want to stay free and cherish what God has done for us. Being set free is the beginning not the end and it is wise to memorise some verses from the Bible to stand upon and to allow these verses to strengthen our faith when temptation arises. We are not alone in this battle the Lord is always with us. Unfortunately, Satan tries to place walls around our lives to limit our effectiveness and reduce our potential to fulfil God's plans and goals for our lives. However, remember that with God we can achieve anything we set out to do.[2]

Sin has a binding hold on the world

Some of the ways that Satan tries to bind us is through sin by condemning us, or by putting doubts in our minds. At these times we refute the doubts by standing on the word of God and remembering we are never condemned in Christ.[3] Indeed, when we confess our sins and ask for forgiveness, God removes our sins as far away as the east is from the west, and He throws those sins into the depths of the ocean.[4] The sin is gone and God has forgotten it, they are no more in His eyes or thoughts.

Nevertheless, if it is sin or past sins that are holding us back from being set free, then it is worth reminding ourselves how a just and righteous God deals with sin and rebellion, because this is of major importance for our understanding of finding God in a broken world. There is a lot of debate around the question of how God deals with sin.[5, 6] Indeed there are quite a number of views on what sin actually consists off and how it can be defined.[7] For our purposes, a working definition of sin is simply missing the mark or falling short of God's perfection or standards.[8] Although I realise that this definition might offend some as being over simplistic, it is a good starting point.

John R. Clarke

Anyone who has been around in the world for a few years will know that mankind is far from being perfect. However, it is popular in some quarters today to think of sin as being different from merely missing the mark or living up to perfection. Some turn to the Ten Commandments when thinking of sin, and in popular thought, murder and adultery are seen as being important violations of God's perfection, but lying and idolatry are considered as being minor sins.[9] When considering sin it is important that we view sin in the same way that God views sin because we will be judged by God's standards not mankinds. The Bible tells us that God destroys those who tell lies,[10] which is a very powerful and overbearing response if lying is only a small violation of His perfection.

We can only conclude that any breach of God's standards is very serious in God's eyes and has severe consequences. Also it is clear that the standards set by humans for categorising sin are not the same as God's, and there is a big gulf between how mankind sees sin and imperfection, and how God views sin.

It should be clear that a loving and caring God views any kind of sin as very serious and in need of rectifying. His word shows us that first and foremost God hates sin.[11,12]

The Bible says God hates sin and will bring His judgment on those who continue to sin. Hate is a very strong word and goes far beyond just being upset or even angry by what men and women do when they sin. The consequences of living a life of disobedience and distain towards God, without repentance and accepting Jesus as Lord and Saviour are clearly spelled out in the Bible, and there will be no excuses for rejecting God's salvation.[13] Separation from God is a unnerving end for any man and that is why it is so important to take sin in our lives seriously. There is a common belief in the Western World today that God has had His day and is irrelevant for 21st Century living but the reality is the opposite, God is needed more today than ever. Just look at the mess the world is in without Him, it is breaking apart and we are only witnessing the beginning of the end, it will become far worse before Christ returns.

We shouldn't be afraid to admit that all of us have at certain times fallen short of the mark and of God's expectations.[14] The Bible tells us that we have strayed away from God and follow our own paths rather than staying on the path God has chosen for us and because of that God has allowed Jesus to take the punishment we deserved on Himself.[15] This is at the centre of the good news of the gospel and we need to remind ourselves what God has done for us and that He waits with open arms to receive us. Guilt is often the biggest obstacle to freedom that we have to overcome. Accepting our failures and the way we are can be a barrier to finding true freedom through Christ.

Will everyone be saved and go to heaven?

A popular view that is gaining in popularity is something called universalism which argues that a loving God would not send men into hell where there is suffering and pain.[16] It is clear from these verses that God is reluctant that anyone perishes and His desire is that all men come to Him and receive forgiveness. God is willing to hold back His judgment to allow enough time for mankind to come to repentance and turn to Him. Indeed, God allowed Israel to remain in captivity in Egypt to allow time for the Amorites to come to repentance.[17] God is waiting and has an allocated time before His second coming. This time is to allow mankind to repent and come to salvation, but the allotted time for the age of the Gentiles will come to an end at God's appointed time.

Therefore, if men and women have not repented and turned to Him, then they will be judged. Yes, it is true that God is merciful and full of grace toward mankind but sin still has to be atoned for and men and women have to choose to accept this grace from God. The reality of the situation is that we were bought at a great price and at a great cost to God.[18]

Indeed there are plenty of verses in the Bible that show that without repentance God's judgement will come on mankind. For example, men hid in caves to try and escape from the wrath of God on the day of judgement;[19] men preferred darkness to coming into the light of Christ and are therefore condemned to their fate;[20] Peter pleaded for men to save themselves from a corrupt generation;[20] we must all stand before God's judgement seat to give an account of what we did in our lives.[21] It is a sobering thought to know what will become of the world that rejects God. However, by accepting Jesus, we are free to enjoy life as God intended throughout eternity. Forever and ever is an extremely long time and the promise of what lies ahead, a life of paradise, is truly amazing and one we cannot fathom.

The problem with universalism is that it aims to release mankind from any obligations or responsibilities. The logical outcome of universalism is that there is no accountability, we can behave exactly as we like because there are no consequences and we are all going to heaven. However, people who believe in universalism and redemption for all are in for an unpleasant surprise because the Bible teaches that we all will be held accountable for what we have done in this life and God hates wickedness.[22]

Make no mistake it is frightening to face the anger and wrath of God without the assurance of the forgiveness of sins through accepting Jesus as Lord and Saviour. God won't be mocked and an important spiritual principle is that men and women will reap what they sow and if that is to reject God and serve the sinful nature then judgement and eternal damnation will follow.[23] For those that accept Jesus as Lord and Saviour and seek to serve God, then they shall be set free.[23]

The difference between the righteous and unrighteous

Jesus told a very important parable to illustrate the difference between the righteous and the unrighteous[24] which serves as a warning for our behaviour even for those who are living within the Kingdom of God. At the centre of the parable are two sets of people those who believe they are serving God and those who are actually serving God. The difference is in how we react to the suffering and needs of others. The righteous help to meet those needs without even thinking about it while the unrighteous let the opportunities pass them by, they are oblivious to the suffering and needs of others. The question then is who are we the righteous or the unrighteous? I know which side I hope to be on.

> ***Don't be a slave to sin but allow the Lord
> to set you free and live in freedom.***

Sin has to be dealt with and the good news is that Jesus has set us free.[25] So don't concern yourself with past sins or failures, move forward with God, and don't let the past ruin what God has planned for your future.

Struggles with sin

For those who struggle with sin and don't seem capable to break free from a persistent or recurring sin, the answer is that Christ has set us free. Ask the Lord for freedom and He will give it freely but it may require persistent and consistent praying. Stand on the promises of God and deliverance will come. Then it is our responsibility to stand firm and not allow sin to re-enter our lives.[26]

Stand firm in the Lord and don't allow yourself to slip back into a life of sin.

We should include the word of God in our prayers when seeking to be set free from repetitive sins in our lives and there are many good examples that we can use to guide our prayers for example Psa 19:13-14.

In the world we often take things for granted but we should always take a few moments to remember who we stand or kneel before when we pray and remember how some of the great saints have felt in the presence of the living God.[27, 28]

We need our lips to be seared with burning coals to cleanse the words of our mouths and our minds and hearts also need to be seared with burning coals to cleanse them from impure thoughts and actions.[27] Praying that the Lord will keep us from sin is an important principle for Christians: in the Lord's Prayer we ask not to be led into temptation and to be delivered from evil.[29]

Remaining free in Christ

In order to remain free from the burden of sin we are required to ask that the Lord continually delivers us from temptation. Do not let darkness dwell in our hearts, bring sin out of darkness into the light, so God can forgive us. Also there is a responsibility on our part to purify ourselves and keep ourselves free from sins.[30] Keep short accounts with God, ask God to forgive us from wilful sins and to deliver us from repeating these very same sins but also ask for forgiveness for the sins that we have committed without even being aware of them.

There is a tendency to try and justify our actions when we do wrong, after all we are only human but this is really self-deception. Be certain that everyone has sinned and we all fall short of God's wonderful standards.[14]

Self-deception is a major hindrance to remaining free in Christ, so always be honest with God about wrongdoings and do not try to hide it because God knows everything and He has promised to remove our failings from us.[31] Confessing our wrongdoings is central to being forgiven for those wrongdoings and there is often a relief that the issue whatever it is has been dealt with and we can move forward with our lives free from the guilt of past wrongdoings. Being forgiven is something to be thankful about and something to rejoice and be happy about. It is surprising how often people feel guilty for being happy and set free. Rejoice in the living God and appreciate what He has done for each of us.

The key is to keep short accounts with God and to confess the things we do wrong regularly. Then victory over sin will come.[32] Part of human nature is to keep feeling guilty for past sins which is holding onto something we have been forgiven for. It is OK to let go of our sin and to move on with freedom not looking back but moving forward in Christ to a new start and a fresh beginning.[3]

We are not condemned and we are free, that is the good news of the gospel of Christ.

Our responsibility with sin doesn't end with asking for forgiveness for our sins. We have the responsibility of forgiving others for their sins against us.[33] This is an important concept because God has promised to forgive us only when we forgive others.

> *Forgiving those that have hurt us is central to being set free from our sins. Without forgiveness in our heart we are not forgiven for the things we have done wrong.*

Forgiving others is vital for our wellbeing and is necessary for us to be forgiven of our sins. Forgiveness is at the heart of the gospel and for some it is difficult to forgive, so deep is the hurt. The good news is that with men some things are impossible but with God all things are possible and with God's help it is possible to forgive even the deepest violations and hurts. Letting go is the hard part and will take time and sometimes a lot of prayer until the release from the past comes and we can truly forgive. Once forgiveness is achieved, where possible we must try and restore the broken relationship.

Let us always seek to be Holy as God is Holy to ask forgiveness for things that we do that mean we fall short of the glory of God. Let us be assured that those who seek forgiveness of their sins before God have been set free through the sacrifice of Christ on the cross. We can move forward with reassurance that Christ has set us free and we are free indeed. Appreciate the freedom God has given us and live free of sin.

A short prayer.

Lord Jesus we are grateful that when we accepted you as Lord and Saviour we came into your Kingdom were there is no condemnation. We come before with the reassurance that when we confess our sins we are forgiven. Dear heavenly Father we thank you for the cross on which our Saviour died and through His blood we are set free from our iniquities and sins. We come before you to confess that we have fallen short of your standards and to ask that you forgive us for our failures. Father we also ask that you will set us free from the sins in our life that still continue to bind us and hinder us from being set free to live the life that you meant us to live. Father we also pray that you help us to forgive others that have hurt us and abused us and caused us pain and grief. Please provide the strength and grace to enable us to forgive and be set free in Jesus name we pray Amen.

6

Overcoming the World

Our purpose in the world

We are here for a purpose and that purpose is to be the Lord's servants on the earth and to play our part in the fulfilment of God's plan. In this we need to know from the outset what we are up against and who we are fighting while we are on the earth.[1]

Firstly, we are involved in a wrestling match, a battle against all the forces that oppose God.[1] Wrestling involves close contact with the forces we are contesting with and at times we will struggle. In wrestling a person seldom stands still and it is a constant battle to get a better grip and hold on the opponent, so that we can overcome and destroy the opponent in victory.

Our enemies are strong, they are rulers, authorities, cosmic powers and spiritual forces.[1] Yet God in His wisdom has pitted us against them but here is the key. He has provided us with the weapons to overcome and have the victory over our enemies. We may not like the idea very much but there is a war between good and evil and we are involved in that war whether we want to be or not. The good news is that God has equipped us with everything we need to fight that war and win it.[2]

God has blessed us and it might seem strange that these blessings are in heaven not on the earth and why has God given us spiritual blessings in the heavenly realms?[2] Because in part that is where the battle is taking place. Also our blessings are safe with God. We must attain to reach into heaven and take hold of the blessings that are there for us. Paul was caught up in the third heaven which he also called paradise and he heard things presumably from God that he could not reveal because he wasn't allowed too.[3] If we want to know the secret things that God has planned (as much as a created being can know the secrets of God) then we need to go to the heavenly places. Incidentally, since there is a third heaven then there has to be a first and second heaven. The first heaven is where God has His throne room.[4] The second heaven is traditionally thought to be where the stars are placed or in the outer atmosphere[5] and an example of the second heaven can be seen when God promised Abraham that He would multiply his descendants, he said they would be as numerous as the stars of heaven.[6] To retrieve our spiritual blessings we have to spiritually enter the heavenly places.

> **To gain our heavenly blessings we have to be lifted up in our spirits into the heavenly places.**

A popular saying of our times is that God's people are so heavenly minded to be no earthly good and I have no idea where this quotation originated from but have included a couple of references here.[7, 8] However, I think the opposite is more likely to be true that we are so earthly minded that we are of very little heavenly use. We are so busy making ends meet and pursuing worldly gain that we have forgotten that we are in a battle to overcome principalities of this dark age.

God has provided the blessings and has equipped us so we are ready for the battle Rulers, powers, authorities and spiritual forces indicate that the enemy is well organised and he has set out his kingdom and dominions to oppose God's. The battle lines are drawn and the war has commenced. Are we ready and aware enough to take our part in this spiritual warfare we have been called to fight and partake in?

When we think of spiritual forces we are reminded of the Special Forces we find in the armed forces of every nation. The SAS in the UK or the US marines. These men and women are specially trained to overcome the enemy no matter what the circumstance. Can we say the same about Christians, are we specially trained? Are we ready to enter the battle? God has equipped us with everything we need to win the earthly battles and the war against evil.

On the US Special Forces web page we will find the quotation "Your most powerful weapon is your mind." [9] This is a starting point and points to the type of weapons we have at our disposal but for the Christian our most powerful weapon is prayer. More than anything else Satan fears powerful, God inspired and God centred prayer.

Weapons of warfare

Let us look at the weapons we have at our disposal, weapons that have divine power.[10] We think of nuclear weapons being the most powerful available to man and talk about the destructive power of nuclear weapons in terms of the number of warheads each weapon carries or the fact that their impact is in the megaton region which is pretty powerful. However, the weapons we are equipped with are divine, their power exceeds anything that man has, yet we very seldom use them. We underestimate the power of prayer and what prayer can achieve. We have everything possible in our armament to defeat the enemy and win the war but we seldom engage the evil head on.

We also need to defend ourselves against the attacks from Satan and therefore it is important to put on the armour of God everyday.[1] The armour is designed to help us stand against the evil that is sure to come against us and protects us from our feet to heads.[1] Out of the armour at our disposal our faith protects us from the accusations and hurtful things that can come our way and the word of God enables us to inflict damage on the enemy.[1]

We often talk about prevention being better than cure,[11] but how often do we seek God about the storms that may be coming for Christians in our nations or the potential threats to our nations. Have we engaged in prayer against the growing threat of lawlessness, or terrorism, or murder, especially murder caused through racism that are beginning to plague some nations? Have we sought God about the things that are on His heart and what are His priorities for our cities, regions and nations? We know that we are growing increasingly closer to the coming of the anti-Christ but as we approach the ever growing days of lawlessness have we sought the Lord regarding what we should be praying for? We are warned to watch and pray and to look for the signs of the coming of the Lord.[12]

Look at some of the examples of victories won through prayer in the Bible, for example Jehoshaphat when God granted an amazing victory over his enemies.[13] Do we believe that God is any less powerful today? Is our nation in trouble? Does it require deliverance? Do we fear for the young people and their future if things are this bad now? Then see what God has promised for those who turn to him in prayer.[14] What God has promised He will bring about and He has promised to answer the prayers of the humble. The promises of God are supernatural promises, in as much as they have divine power. What God has promised He will bring about, make no mistake we are on the winning side.

The strongholds of Satan

In thinking about what needs to be changed and defeated we need to think about what the Bible means when it talks about the strongholds of Satan?[10] What are the arguments and every lofty opinion raised against the knowledge of God? What are the thoughts that need to be taken captive?

There are many strongholds in the world and these are mind-sets that set themselves up to oppose God and what He has revealed in the Bible. There are too many strongholds to list them all here as they would take a separate book by themselves but here are a few of the more common strongholds that try to bind up the world.

On a spiritual realm biblical criticism comes near the top of the list. This is the mind-set that questions that the Bible is the word of God and then questions everything relating to its authenticity and its authority. At the centre of biblical criticism is the question "Did God really say that?" It is not a new question, it is as old as Adam and Eve and the fall from the Garden of Eden. Why is Satan still using it? Because it works. Its primary purpose is to put doubt into the believer's heart that the Bible is not the true word of God and that it is full of flaws, and that in turn paralyses some believers, and indeed some churches and denominations from entering the battle. The word of God, the Bible, is the sword of Spirit and has the ability to cut between the soul and the spirit.[1, 15] When Jesus came under attack from Satan He defended Himself with the word of God and hence why the Bible comes in for special attention from Satan, because through the word of God, Satan was defeated.[16]

If we resist the devil he will flee from us.[17] Satan is afraid of us. If we stand on the word of God we will be victorious but not if we have doubts. We have more power invested in us than we believe.[18] Claim the promise and think and believe what it is like to be able to do all things, to be victorious in all things through Christ

Other strongholds include communism, a mind-set that looks for utopia and fulfilment on earth and has rejected the existence of God. Karl Marx was quoted as calling religion the opium of the people. A former Russian President Khrushchev once said, "We have been into space but didn't see God" although it was said that it was the Astronaut Gregarin that actually first uttered these words.[19] Everything about communism opposes God because communism tries to convince us that we can set up paradise (utopia) on the earth without God. In communism, the state replaces God.

Consumerism, the need to have possessions in order to be happy and fulfilled is contrary to what the Bible states. There is nothing wrong with having possessions in themselves but when individuals over spend in order to be happy then there is something amiss.

Capitalism which is an economic system in which investment in and ownership of the means of production, distribution, and exchange of wealth is made and maintained chiefly by private individuals or corporations, especially as contrasted to cooperatively or state-owned means of wealth.[20] The stronghold of capitalism is that fulfilment can be achieved through the creation of wealth. God's word tells us otherwise.[21]

Who do we believe the word of God or the word of Governments who are pushing Capitalism as the solution to the world's problems?

Evolution is another stronghold that states that all life evolved from a primeval soup so there is no creation and therefore no God. As stated earlier, there are many more strongholds that warrant a whole book but they all have one thing in common and that is they seek to replace or to undermine God because without God there is no accountability.

The word of God our most powerful weapon

The word of God is a powerful and our most important weapon because it is what God has equipped us with for our endeavours in the world. Therefore, it is important that we not only know the word of God but can use the word to defend ourselves when we come under attack and temptation.[16]

Our weapons are the word of God, the Blood of the Lamb and the testimony of the Saints.[22]

The word of God is living and active and sharper than any two-edged sword, able to pierce between the soul and the spirit of man and able to discern the thoughts and intentions of men;[15] the word is like a hammer that breaks rock to pieces;[23] we are called to live by the word of God;[24] The word of God is also our main weapon for the battle against evil[25] and finally everything that is contained in the Bible is to enable us to understand who we and where we stand in God.[26]

> **We overcome Satan by the word of God, the Blood of the Lamb and the power of our testimony.[22]**

The word of God is vital for our own protection and for our victory over the world. It is essential that we study it because it is the lifeblood of all Christians. Know the word of God and love the word of God because someday it will save our lives.

The Blood of the Lamb

The accuser of the brethren is Satan and he accuses us day and night before God asking for our souls and to sift us like wheat but we have already conquered him.[27]

Through the Blood of the Lamb we have our sins forgiven;[28] we have been bought by Him and the currency He used was His own Blood;[29] we are part of God's family and have changed from being enemies of God into being joined with God.[29] For those who have fallen out with partners or family members it is a relief to be reconciled and have the relationship restored. It is also important to know that we are forgiven from the past and can look forward with confidence to the future.[30] We are clean and pure in the eyes of God and for most of us that is vital to our sense of well-being.[29, 30] God has paid the ransom to set us free and we can claim that promise every moment of every day.[31, 32]

Whenever we fall into sin and repent it is the Blood of Christ that makes us clean and acceptable to God.

Our testimony

We also stand by the word of our testimony. What has God done for us, do we truly grasp how deep, wide and high the love of God is?

Our testimony is knowing what Christ has rescued us from, knowing where we are going, and who we are in Him. We have abundant life;[33] we can live above the troubles and not let them worry us.[34] Nobody can oppose us, we are more than conquerors and we are inseparable from God.[35]

Do we believe who we are in Christ because that is the key to victorious Christian living, the key to winning the war.[36]

We should dare to have the dreams of heaven and of the victory over the world and any adversity we are facing because that is our position and right in Christ. So often we shrink away from the battle or are afraid of our circumstances and allow them to cloud our judgment and dictate our futures. The reality is that we are free and we are a lot more powerful than we think we are. We are capable and able enough to pull down strongholds because God has equipped us to do so.

God has given us authority to trample on serpents and scorpions and power over all the enemy and nothing can hurt us or harm us without His permission.[37] We have grounds for rejoicing and being glad because we are part of God's family and nothing can take that away from us.[38]

We are overcomers through Christ and we follow where Christ has gone before. So take heart, we can overcome the world and everything the world can throw at us. That is our testimony and that is our position in Christ and nothing but absolutely nothing can erase that or damage that position.

A short prayer

Father we thank you that you love us so much that you have equipped us with every spiritual blessing in the heavenly realms and have provided with weapons of warfare to take down every stronghold that comes against the word of God. Nothing but nothing can stand against the word of God, the Blood of the Lamb and the testimony of the saints. Lord Jesus show us who we are in you and give us the confidence and the belief to know that nothing can separate us from your love. Not even the gates of hell can stand against the church of God, Amen come Lord Jesus.

7

Victorious living

Learning to be victorious

The first step in victorious living is to develop a grateful and a thankful heart for all that God has done for us. A central part of victorious Christian living is to make God the focus of our lives, the centre of our hearts and to meditate and think about what God has done for us continually.

The battle begins in our minds because what we believe is entrenched in our minds and Satan will try to get us to doubt God and to make us unsure of what we believe and hope for and his tactic is often to challenge us with 'Did God really say that?'. That is why it is so important to stand on the word of God. Whenever we have to make big decisions that affect our lives and families lives we need to be able to stand on the word of God. It is important to receive a word from God, pray it through until will obtain the peace of God so that when the attack from our enemy comes, we can stand in assurance on the word that the Lord has already imparted in our hearts. When Jesus was tempted in the wilderness He overcome Satan by the word of God.[1] Man doesn't live on food alone but He lives by the word of God and not just the word of God but every word of God.[2] Having a verse or a passage of the Bible that reassures us that what we are doing is the God's chosen path for us, is vital, because Satan will try to dislodge us from that path using any devious means that he can.

To live a life of victory we need to change our worldly mind-set, such as being ambitious, being successful in terms of having possessions, and becoming financially rich, and align our thoughts and objectives with those of God.[3] What are God's desires for us? It is not something we hear a lot about today for some reason, but God desires that we become like His son Jesus. We are called to be imitators of God and indeed our whole purpose for being on the earth is to be a reflection of what the Son of God is like.[4] God desires we begin to reflect the character of Jesus in the way we talk, the way we behave, and the way we conduct ourselves in our everyday lives. The challenge is to set our thinking so it is more aligned with God's thinking and so enable His Kingdom to grow on the earth.[5]

In the world but not a part of the world

God has called us to be in the world without being like the world which can be a challenge when everyone around us is chasing after worldly things. Even when watching Christian programmes we can be challenged. Just think about this for a moment when was the last time we heard someone say that God wants to make us rich? Now think of the last time we heard anyone in a Christian television programme say take up your cross and follow me? Becoming rich is very popular in some avenues of Christianity but having to take up a heavy cross and follow in the footsteps of Christ is not popular in our day, and that is extremely worrying because it is at the centre of the Gospel message. Remember that the disciples were astonished by Jesus' teaching relating to rich men and questioned who then can be saved.[6] Jesus answer was that all things are possible with God.[7] Do we believe that nothing is impossible for God? How big is our God and how great is He in our thinking, what do we believe Him for and how do we conduct our daily living? God is able to bring about a transformation in our lives if we are willing to allow Him access to all areas of our lives.

There may be areas of our lives that we don't want to surrender to God, we like those areas and we don't want to hand them over to the living God. I had a friend who was scared to surrender all of her life to God because she was worried that God would send her to be a missionary in a dangerous part of the world. God will not test us beyond what we can cope with. In my experience God only sends people to be missionaries who have a heart's desire to serve God in that way. Surrendering our lives to the Lord is the safest way forward because by surrendering our life it will be saved.[8]

Because of the danger of being tempted away from the Gospel message by the riches of the world, the Lord warns us to be vigilant regarding what enters our heart because the spring of life flows out of it.[9]

There is much to be thankful for and remember when Peter was walking on the water he began to sink when he took his eyes off Jesus and looked at the storm around him. Develop a positive heart and mind and know that we can achieve whatever we strive for if it is the same things that God wants for our lives.[10] There is nothing that we cannot accomplish if we believe and have faith in God to achieve it through us.[11]

Prayer the secret of our success

The big question is how do we know for sure that what we are asking for is the will of God or is in line with God's purposes? The answer lies often in our own hearts because when things are not of God or in line with God's purposes then we feel uneasy and not at peace. There is something inside of us that warns us that we are out of alignment with God's will. The peace of God guides our lives and without His peace we know that what we are praying for is not His will for us. Another test of whether what we are praying for is the will of God, is what we are praying for, in line with the word of God? Do we have Bible verses to back up what we are asking for then take hold of the promises of God to support our prayer?

Once we have a verse to support our prayer request hold onto that prayer with all of our hearts because the answer will come in God's way and in His time.[12] Have faith in God and believe, that is the key to victorious Christian living, never take our eyes off Jesus keep Him in focus at all times.

Develop our thought life so that it is focused, rooted and grounded in the word of God so we can say with the Psalmist that our thoughts and goals are the same as God's goals and thoughts.[13]

Focus on the thoughts of God as they are revealed to us in the Bible because they are precious and we will find peace, comfort, rest and inspiration in them.

Praise is a requirement for victorious living

Praising and worshipping God is vital to victorious Christian living. Those who worship the Lord must do so with their spirit and the most meaningful worship happens when our spirit is joined with God's Spirit and moves into the heavenly places.[14] Worship that meets with God is revigorating and changes our whole perspective on life and the challenges we may be facing. It renews us in our inner most being and lifts us to a new understanding of who God is. The problems of the world all seem to evaporate and are placed into perspective of how small they actually are. We gain a renewed love for God and are realigned and re-joined to Him in a way that cannot be explained in words.

What can we worship and praise Him for? Take time to notice His creation and all the breath-taking things that flow out of the vastness and beauty of nature, the landscapes, the beautiful sunrises and sunsets.[15] I used to watch birds in my spare time and I was taken back by the enormous diversity in nature and all the different varieties of birds that brighten up the environments we live in. The sheer wonder of discovering something new and so beautiful that I've never noticed or seen before. I'm forever shaken with the sheer power of nature such as, lightning during a powerful thunder storm, the waves slashing against rocks on a windy day or the television programmes showing the eruptions of volcanoes or what it is like in space and the universe we live in.

Praise can be a vehicle to release all the tensions and frustrations that we feel as well as being something we can do spontaneously and not just when we attend church or a spiritual meeting or conference. We can praise Him with everything we have for no other reason than we want too.[16] Praise him because of His love for us and that despite everything we do or don't do, His love for us continues and never ends.[17]

Praise Him because He strengthens us, renews us and revitalises us.[18] Praise Him regardless of our circumstances.[19] Praise and worship Him for who He is,[20] or just for what He has done for us.[21] The best and most wonderful time to praise God is when things have not gone the way we hoped and we are feeling upset.[22]

There are numerous reasons for worshipping and praising God and as soon as we do, difficulties or adverse circumstances can be overcome.

We can praise God for being our rock and our fortress and for leading us and guiding us.[23] We can thank Him that our sins are forgiven and He has forgotten them.[24] We can be thankful to God for the way He guides us and leads us and provides counsel for the way forward.[25] In fact we should praise God in all circumstances just because He is worthy.

When we come into a place where we are alone with God, free from interruption and when we earnestly seek God and we feel His presence with us then true worship can take place.[26] Pour out our hearts to Him and He will meet our every need.

It is not coincidence that the longest book in the Bible is the book of Psalms that reflects and expresses the worship and praise of God. Also the book of Psalms is placed at the centre of God's word to us. The last word in the book of Psalms is to praise the Lord and keep on praising the Lord.[27]

Praise and worship has the effect of lifting us up into the heavenly places, high above the storms of the earth. However, don't think or believe we are a failure if we are overwhelmed by the battles and struggles that arise in the world and find praise is hard or difficult. Being a Christian does not make us anything less than human and we all experience difficult moments, days, months and periods in our lives. Don't allow the past to destroy the future.

Have faith

The third element for victorious Christian living is to have faith in God and the definition of faith is to have an assurance that what we hope for will happen and take place before we see them.[28] Hebrews chapter 11 has many examples of people who had faith, and believed God for things that had not yet come into being, and some of them like Abraham never saw the fruition of their faith in their own lifetimes. Sometimes it is difficult to keep on believing when everything around us is telling us otherwise, but when the storm is at its height is the very time when breakthrough faith occurs. The darkest part of the night is often the hours leading up to dawn. It is at this point that we need to continue believing and to never give up. Considering Abraham, some of the answers to prayers may not come until we are in heaven.[29] The promises of God are not restricted to this earthly life, and the best answers to our faith, our hopes and our prayers may not come to fruition until we are in the presence of God in heaven.

Faith is important because without faith we cannot believe God can do what He says He can, so prayer and hope become futile without faith. We cannot please God without having faith.[30] Therefore, it may be useful to make a list of the things that we have faith for, so that in the difficult times we can reflect on our list and gain encouragement in the those things that form the basis of our faith.

Some of the things that are easy to add to our list may include; we believe that Jesus is our Lord and Saviour and all that call on His name will be saved and we believe that God is faithful and answers our prayers, when we pray we are to place all our worries in His hands.[31] When you think about it probably the safest and best place for our worries and the things that trouble us is in the hands of God. Make a list of things we have faith in, and we may be surprised to see how many things we can add to our list. We may be very surprised at how much faith we actually have and what we are actually already trusting and believing God for. Then we should review the list regularly and see how many answers to prayer have come when we have had faith and belief in God to bring them into being.

Every day we can choose to live a life of faith and belief in Christ[32] and this can change our perspective on what is happening in the world around us and with good reason when you consider the storms we can see occurring all around us. Remember the currency of heaven is faith which is more valuable than gold.[33]

We are called to overcome the world and this can be a struggle and a battle but we overcome the world by having faith in Jesus our Lord and through this we have the victory.[34]

Study the Bible because our faith increases through reading and listening to the word of God,[35] and the Lord through the Holy Spirit often speaks to us through His word. Also His word strengthens us for each day's challenges and tests that we may face. It is always a blessing to meet and talk with Christians that truly know the word of God. The word of God will transform our lives.

What are our responsibilities for victorious Christian living apart from transforming our minds, developing a life of praise and worship and having faith in God? Victorious living comes to those who strive to keep the promises of God and with such people God promises to make His home.[36] To have the Lord make His home with us and live with us should give us great reassurance of our position in

God. The Lord is forever with us and is closer than we think and believe. As individuals we may think at times that we are weak and have little power to influence matters but that is not what the Bible tells us. In reality we are a chosen, Holy people, we are royalty, dedicated to God.[37] The Lord has provided us with all the power of heaven, and every blessing, and every weapon necessary to ensure the victory.

There will be a day when the Lord wipes away every tear and all our heartache and temptations will be gone and a thing of the past.[38] Praise the Lord for that. It is God's deepest longing that He shall be our God and we shall be His people, His family, His children.[39] The very good news is that Jesus is coming back soon to take those who belong to Him to heaven to be with Him forever and ever.[40] There will be nothing experienced on this earth that even comes close to being in heaven with God. There is no language that can begin to describe the beauty and sheer awe of being in the heavenly places.

We are longing to meet the Lord and for Him to say to us, well my good and faithful servant you have used what little you had to further my Kingdom.[41] Come be with me and take your reward. We can and will live the victorious Christian life because it is our destiny and our calling to do so. We may not be rich as the world measures riches, in terms of material possessions and wealth. However, we will be extremely rich in heaven because of our ever increasing faith in the Lord Jesus and the belief and perseverance we are developing no matter what the challenges of life are.

We all love a happy ending but God through our Lord and Saviour Jesus offers us a happy beginning that will last for eternity.

The Lord is coming back soon, each new day His return gets nearer, come Lord Jesus.[42]

A short prayer

Dear Lord Jesus we are so blessed that you have chosen us before the foundation of the earth to share eternity with you. It is humbling to think, who are we, that you would chose us out of all the world. We come before you in true awe and reverence and praise that we should have our names written in the Lamb's book of life. Father teach us to number our days aright and to be truly grateful for all that you have done for us. We ask that you would strengthen us and bless us and make your face to shine upon us so that we would truly have an intimate relationship with you. In learning to move forward in victorious Christian living teach us to focus our love and attention upon heavenly things and especially on you, so that we may truly grasp how high and deep and wide is your love for us. Help us to truly know that if you are for us nothing can stand against us. In Jesus name we pray, Amen

REFERENCES

Chapter 1: Embracing the love of God

[1]   Source Center for Disease Control and Prevention available at http://www.cdc.gov/nchs/nvss/marriage_divorce_tables.htm (accessed June 2015)

[2]   Source The Daily Mail available online at http://www.dailymail.co.uk/health/article-2356902/Prozac-Nation-Use-antidepressants-UK-soared-500-past-20-years.html (accessed June 2015)

[3]   The Science of love available at: http://www.youramazingbrain.org/lovesex/sciencelove.htm (accessed June 2015)

[4]   John 3:16

[5]   Habb 1:2-4

[6]   Rev 6:9-10

[7]   Matt 13:24-30

[8]   2 Pet 3:9

[9]   Eph 3:18-19

[10] Psa 80:3, 7,19

[11] Rom 8:38-39

[12] Rom 12:2

[13] Jer 32:38

[14] 2 Cor 13:4-8

[15] 1 John 4:8

John R. Clarke

Chapter 2: God's plan for our lives

1 Prov 16:3
2 Jer 29:11
3 Eze 37:27
4 Gen 3:8-12
5 Deut 8:2
6 Heb 13:8
7 Luke 15: 11-32
8 John 6:16-21
9 Matt 7:24-27
10 Gen 2:16-17
11 Jonah 2
12 Isa 1:18-20
13 John 3:36
14 Matt 7:13-14
15 Luke 23:39-43
16 Rev 6:15-17
17 John 1:12
18 2 Pet 3:9
19 Tentmaker available at: http://www.tentmaker.org/articles/savior-of-the-world/all-saved.htm (accessed June 2015)
20 Rev 6, 8 and 9
21 Rev 7
22 Rom 10:13
23 1 John 2:12
24 Eph 1:13-14
25 John 14:16-21
26 John 3:16
27 John 14:21-23
28 Matt 16:24

29 John 15:20

30 Eph 6:12

31 Isa 43:2

Chapter 3: Be Holy as I am Holy

1 Baker's Evangelical Dictionary of Biblical Theology. Holy, holiness available at: http://www.biblestudytools.com/dictionaries/bakers-evangelical-dictionary/holy-holiness.html (accessed June 2015)

2 1 Pet 1:16

3 John 1:12

4 John 8:36

5 Rom 10:13

6 Rom 8:1

7 Rom 7:15-18

8 Rom 6:23

9 John 14:23

10 Phil 1:6

11 1 Thess 4:17

12 Gal 5:13

13 Gal 5:19-22

14 Mark 10:8

15 1 Corinth 6:18

16 1 Corinth 6:9

17 TheFreeDictionary.com available at: http://www.thefreedictionary.com/idolatry (accessed June 2015)

18 1 Tim 6:10

19 Prov 10:22

20 Phil 4:20

21 Phil 1:6

22 Gal 6:22-24

23 Matt 22:36-40

24 Luke 1:37

[25] Matt 13:44-46

[26] Rev 7:9-17

[27] Psa 37:4-6

Chapter 4: *The fruit of the Spirit*

[1] Fruit nutrition facts available at: http://www.nutrition-and-you.com/fruit-nutrition.html (accessed June 2015)

[2] Gal 5:22-24

[3] Matt 22:36-40

[4] 1 Corinth 13:1-2

[5] John 15:1-14

[6] 1 Corinth 13: 4-8

[7] Mark 12:30-31

[8] Matt 12:31

[9] Mic 7:18-19

[10] Neh 8:10

[11] Rev 2:4

[12] Psa 30:4-5

[13] Jam 1:2-4

[14] John 16:22-24

[15] Rom 12:12

[16] Isa 14:31

[17] Prov 16:24; Prov 15:1; Prov 15:23

[18] Corrie Ten Boom, John Sherrill, Elizabeth Sherrill. The hiding place. Chosen Books, Michigan, USA, 2015

[19] Daily Mail. The infidelity epidemic: Never have marriage vows been under so much strain. available at http://www.dailymail.co.uk/news/article-2311947/The-infidelity-epidemic-Never-marriage-vows-strain-Relationship-expert-Kate-Figes-spent-3-years-finding-adultery-worryingly-common.html (accessed June 2015)

[20] Rev 2:10

[21]   Psa 31:23

[22]   2 Corinth 5:17

[23]   The Guardian. Hospital patients complain of rude staff, lack of compassion and long waits. Available at: http://www.theguardian.com/society/2011/feb/23/hospital-patients-rude-staff-long-waits (accessed June 2015)

[24]   The Nursing Times. Ethical and compassionate nursing supplement. Available at: http://www.nursingtimes.net/Journals/2011/08/24/j/y/s/NT-Ethical--Compassionate-Care.pdf (accessed June 2015)

[25]   Anne-Marie Rafferty. We can read Nightingale as a credo for compassion today. The Nursing Times. Ethical and compassionate nursing supplement page 3. Available at: http://www.nursingtimes.net/Journals/2011/08/24/j/y/s/NT-Ethical--Compassionate-Care.pdf (accessed June 2015)

[26]   Alys Cole-King & Paul Gilbert. Compassionate care: the theory and the reality. J Holistic Healthcare 2011;8:29-36.

[27]   The Guardian. Europe faces 'colossal humanitarian catastrophe' of refugees dying at sea. Available at: http://www.theguardian.com/world/2014/jun/02/europe-refugee-crisis-un-africa-processing-centres (accessed June 2015)

[28]   BBC News Website. Why is EU struggling with migrants and asylum? Available at: http://www.search.ask.com/web?q=refugees+and+North+Africa&apn_dtid=%5EOSJ000%5EYY%5EGB&apn_dbr=ie_11.0.9600.17126&psv=&itbv=12.21.0.114&p2=%5EBBE%5EOSJ000%5EYY%5EGB&apn_pt_nrs=BBE&o=APN11406&gct=hp&tpid=ORJ-SPE&pf=V7&trgb=IE&pt=tb&apn_uid=604C6ADF-BC50-4EBE-8A6B-6852761A113A&tpr=1&doi=2014-12-31&ts=1434130008226 (accessed June 2015)

29   1Pet 3:15; 2 Tim 2:24; Titus 3:2

30   Matt 28:19-20

31   2 Pet 1:5-9

Chapter 5: Christ has set you free

1   Psa 107:1-43

2   Phil 4:13

3   Rom 8:1-2

4   Psa 103:12, Mic 7:19

5   William Lane Craig vs Ray Bradley. Can a loving God send people to hell? available at: http://www.reasonablefaith.org/can-a-loving-god-send-people-to-hell-the-craig-bradley-debate (accessed June 2015)

6   Debate.org. Does God punish sinners for eternity? Available at: http://www.debate.org/opinions/does-god-punish-sinners-for-eternity (accessed June 2015)

7   Wikipedia. Christian views on sin. Available at: https://en.wikipedia.org/wiki/Christian_views_on_sin (accessed June 2015)

8   Bible tools. Bible verses about sin missing the mark. Available at: http://www.bibletools.org/index.cfm/fuseaction/Topical.show/RTD/cgg/ID/6773/Sin-as-Missing-Mark.htm (accessed June 2015)

9   Deut 5:1-21

10   Psa 6:5

11   Psa 5:4-5

12   Psa 11:5-7

13   Rom 6:23

14   Rom 3:23

15   Isa 53:6

16   Christian Apologetics and Research Ministry. 1Tim 2:4, 2 Pet 3:9, and universalism. Available at: https://carm.

org/1-tim-24-2-pet-39-and-universalism (accessed June 2015)

17 Gen 15:13-16
18 John 3:16-21
19 Rev 6:15-17
20 Acts 2:38-41
21 2 Cor 5:10
22 Isa 59:2-3
23 Gal 6:7-8
24 Matt 25:31-46
25 John 8:34-36
26 Gal 5:1
27 Isa 6:5
28 Rev 1:9-18
29 Matt 6:13
30 2 Cor 7:1
31 1 John 1:7-9
32 1 Cor 15:56-57
33 Luke 17:1-4, Matt 6:14-15

Chapter 6: Overcoming the world

1 Eph 6:12-18
2 Eph 1:3
3 2 Cor 12:2
4 Rev 5:1
5 Bible Knowledge.com. Warning do not engage with demons in the 2nd heaven unless directly authorized by the Lord. Available at: http://www.bible-knowledge.com/engaging-with-demons-in-the-2nd-heaven/ (accessed June 2015)
6 Gen 22:17
7 Saints gone wild. 11. Heavenly Minded and Earthly Good (1 Corinthians 3:18-4:5). Available at: https://bible.org/

seriespage/11-heavenly-minded-and-earthly-good-1-corinthians-318-45 (accessed June 2015)

8 Peter Wallace. Col 3:1-7 "So Heavenly Minded that You Are No Earthly Good" available at: http://peterwallace.org/sermons/col31.htm (accessed June 2015)

9 Your most powerful weapon is your mind. Available at: http://www.goarmy.com/special-forces.html (accessed June 2015)

10 2 Cor 10:3-6

11 The Free Dictionary. Available at: http://idioms.thefreedictionary.com/Prevention+is+better+than+cure (accessed June 2015)

12 Luke 21:36

13 2 Chron 20

14 2 Chron 7:14-15

15 Heb 4:12

16 Matt 4:1-11

17 Jam 4:7-8

18 Phil 4:13

19 Space theology (astrotheology). Available at: http://spacetheology.blogspot.co.uk/2011/09/yuri-gagarin-and-god.html (accessed June 2015)

20 The Free Dictionary.com. Capitalism. Available at: http://www.thefreedictionary.com/capitalism (accessed June 2015)

21 Matt 19:24

22 Rev 12:11

23 Jer 23:29

24 Matt 4:4

25 Eph 6:17

26 2 Tim 3:16-17

27 Luke 22:31-32

28 Rom 3:25

29 Eph 1:7
30 Heb 9:14
31 Heb 10:22
32 Rev 5:9-10
33 John 10:10
34 John 14:1
35 Rom 8:31-39
36 1 Cor 2:9
37 Luke 10:19
38 Luke 10:18-20; Rev 12:9

Chapter 7: Victorious living

1   Matt 4:1-11
2   Matt 4:4
3   Rom 12:2
4   Eph 5:1-2
5   Eph 4:22-24
6   Matt 19:25
7   Matt 19:26
8   Matt 16:24-27
9   Prov 4:23
10 Phil 4:13
11 Mark 9:23
12 Matt 21:22
13 Psa 139:17
14 John 4:24
15 Psa 71:8
16 Psa 103:1
17 1 Chron 16:34
18 Psa 73:25-26
19 Hab 3:17-18
20 2 Sam 7:22
21 Psa 105:1

22   Psa 42:11
23   Psa 23
24   Psa 32:1
25   Psa 32:7
26   Psa 62:1-8
27   Psa 150:6
28   Heb 11:1
29   Heb 11:12
30   Heb 11:6
31   1 Pet 5:7; Phil 4:6
32   2 Cor 5:7; Hab 2:4
33   1 Pet 1:7
34   1 John 5:4
35   Rom 10:17
36   John 14:21-23
37   1 Pet 2:9
38   Rev 21:4
39   Deut 6:6
40   Rev 22:12-13
41   Matt 25:31-33
42   Rev 22:20

Printed in the United States
By Bookmasters